COURAGE TO LOVE...
When Your Marriage Hurts

COURAGE TO LOVE...

When Your Marriage Hurts

GERALD FOLEY

AVE MARIA PRESS
NOTRE DAME, INDIANA 46556

Excerpts from Dan Morris, "Seasons of a Marriage," reprinted with permission from U.S. CATHOLIC, published by Claretian Publications, 205 W. Monroe St., Chicago, IL 60606.

Scripture selections from The New American Bible Copyright © 1970 by the Confraternity of Christian Doctrine, Washington, DC, are all used with permission of the copyright owner. All rights reserved.

© 1992 by Ave Maria Press, Notre Dame, IN 46556

International Standard Book Number: 0-87793-488-6
Library of Congress Catalog Card Number: 92-71816
Cover and text design by Katherine Robinson Coleman
Printed and bound in the United States of America.

CONTENTS

PROLOGUE

"A lot of people get divorced who really don't want to," says Sandy. She and Mark were parted for two years.

"We still had feelings for each other," adds Mark, "and I knew we belonged together, but we had problems with our marriage. We felt we were the only ones with problems until we listened to others and realized they'd gotten themselves back together and were able to sit down and discuss and dialogue."

Mark and Sandy reconciled after experiencing the Retrouvaille program in Chicago. Retrouvaille is a successful and important ministry to hurting marriages now rapidly taking root in more and more cities across North America and elsewhere. After I witnessed their remarriage in the presence of their children and first grandchild, Sandy wrote: "There is no explaining how it works—the important thing is that it works. We believe in it strongly enough that we gave a sizeable donation from the sale of our house to the organization that saved our home."

People like Mark and Sandy were the seeds for this book, but I have chosen not to write a book specifically about Retrouvaille. Rather, building upon some of its insights, I have attempted a book to help hurting couples find hope for their relationship. Since every married couple goes through difficult moments in their relationship, I trust the book will speak to couples who are surviving well in marriage as well as those who are floundering.

I have always hesitated to write about marriage since I am a priest and unmarried. However, after thirty years of counseling, listening to thousands of couples tell their stories, and working closely with several marriage ministries, I have a perspective drawn from the shared experience of people living in relationships.

I start the book with a chapter on Retrouvaille because this ministry has shaped many of my insights, and because I believe it is one of the best helps for hurting couples today. I wish that every couple struggling in their marriage could experience the Retrouvaille program. Something happens when other couples tell their stories to help us reflect on our own. Since many couples cannot share this experience, due to the limited number of Retrouvaille programs available or an inability to participate in such programs, I offer stories and insights based on the Retrouvaille experience.

Each chapter ends with a reflection question and a sharing question. You might use the reflection question to see how the ideas presented relate to your life. The sharing questions can help you focus on your own experiences, especially by sharing with your spouse or with a group of couples. Sharing questions, hopes, and disappointments can be very healing.

My special thanks to Bruce and Marg Bridger and Fr. John Vella, who first called me to Retrouvaille after shepherding its beginnings in Canada. They planted the seed, which has been nurtured by team couples and priests as well as the hurting couples who have participated in Retrouvaille. You will meet some of them in this book. They give me faith in marriage. They also remind me over and over how beautiful people are. In a divorce-riddled society, where families are often victims, they call me to believe that, as Robert Kennedy said, "One man with courage is a majority."

PART I

RESOURCES FOR TROUBLED MARRIAGES

1

Sources of Hope

I was on a United Airlines flight to Chicago. A headline in the airline's magazine struck me. It said: "You're Never the Same Once You Know You Can Change the World." Convinced we need to make some changes in our world, I read the full-page ad. It turned out to be an advertisement for *Playboy*, which stated that the readers of this magazine are shaping today's society. I found myself getting angry as I read the article, thinking that we needed to save people from the *Playboy* philosophy.

I wanted to save people by creating an environment for marriage better than the mood of our secular culture. As director of a diocesan Catholic Charities organization and pastor of a country parish, I had spent much of my time with couples in marital difficulties. I enjoyed marriage counseling, but, like most counselors, felt disillusioned with the slow healing process and the overwhelming need. I began to realize that there were other people who shared my dream of changing the world when I attended a Marriage Encounter weekend in January, 1972.

After the experience, I sent many couples in counseling to Marriage Encounter when I thought their relationship was stable enough. Most had a good weekend, and were certainly helped by Marriage Encounter. Some were even selected as teams to present these weekends, whether they were ready or not. I always asked couples to continue counseling, but many dropped out when they thought their marital difficulties were now behind them. As a result, many of them crashed within a few weeks, feeling even more miserable now that their hopes were dashed again.

Marriage Encounter is a great program, directed toward strengthening already intact marriages. But team couples in the 1970s were already concerned that many participants had communication and relationship problems beyond the scope of a Marriage Encounter weekend. Several of these team couples in Hull, Quebec were asked to adapt their Marriage Encounter talks and present a weekend for hurting marriages. Led by Guy and Jeannine Beland, Retrouvaille was first presented in the French language in Hull, Quebec in July, 1977.

The first weekend in the English language was presented in Toronto in October, 1978. Soon after, the French efforts died in Quebec, leaving Toronto as the only city offering this ministry. By 1981, both Toronto and Sudbury were offering regular weekends, with people coming long distances to participate.

Initially, Marriage Encounter sponsor couples agreed to provide "couple-to-couple" support after the weekend. The ultimate goal was to bridge these couples into one of the Marriage Encounter support groups. However, couples needed more help than provided by the early format based on an adapted Marriage Encounter.

Fr. John Vella and Marg and Bruce Bridger headed up an effort to revise the contents of the weekend and develop a post-weekend follow-up in 1981. Professionals helped the Retrouvaille teams to develop a new content and format for this ministry. The response to the new format was overwhelming. By 1982 the Toronto community was convinced their program could help hurting couples, and a survey of participants confirmed their conviction. Eager to share Retrouvaille with others around the world, they held expansion conferences that year in Halifax, Vancouver, Chicago, and Los Angeles for interested dioceses.

Retrouvaille is a ministry of couples and priests who share concern for couples experiencing difficulties in marriage. It begins with a weekend given by three couples and a priest, who are present not as counselors but as peer ministers. The team members share their own experiences, letting participants know how they found help within themselves for their painful marriages. This is not a problem-solving ministry but a relationship-building ministry. The goal of the weekend is to get husbands and wives to communicate with each other at the feeling level. Most likely, it's been a long time since they have communicated at this depth—if they ever have.

Jane and Bob attended Retrouvaille in Rapid City. "We were told that you're ready for the pain of recovery when the pain of living with the problem is too great," claims Jane. "By going, you are admitting that your marriage really has some issues that are too painful to deal with any other way."

"In Retrouvaille, we heard other couples talk about their marital problems," Bob commented. "Hearing the team couples discuss their own relationships—the kind of pain they have experienced and the resolutions that took place through the commitment they made to each other at the Retrouvaille weekend—really moved a lot of people at the weekend."

"In ten or fifteen years of marriage a lot of pain can accumulate. A lot of unresolved issues get swept under the rug, but they're still there. To hear other couples talking about having the courage to roll the carpet back and deal with those painful issues really gave us courage to do it too," Jane concluded.

Participants make an initial three month commitment to Retrouvaille. They did not get into trouble in one weekend, nor is one weekend enough to break the habits of behavior and attitudes that resulted in their drifting apart in the first place. Three months of post-weekend sessions provide an opportunity for couples to strengthen their new-found awareness of one another. These follow-up sessions reinforce concepts learned on the weekend, challenging couples to make the changes that will enable them to rebuild their relationship.

Couples are then invited to continue in CORE (Continuing Our Retrouvaille Experience), a support group for those who feel they need further help. While Retrouvaille does not try to hang onto couples indefinitely, experience suggests that without support to continue change and growth, couples easily slip back into old patterns of behavior. The ultimate goal is to get couples into support groups with other stable couples, such as Marriage Encounter, Christian Family Movement, or parish groups.

Retrouvaille does not have a strong denominational thrust. Rather, it tries to foster a deep awareness of the God who calls us to be channels of God's grace. "We do not hold prayer sessions or teach religion," state Bruce and Marg Bridger, who led the efforts to develop this ministry. "But we do promote the belief that God is a vital necessity and should be an integral part of every Christian marriage relationship."

Presenting couples and priests have an honest desire to help struggling couples free themselves from pain and bitterness. Because of their own journey, they understand the difficulty of the participants and reach out to them with empathy. Retrouvaille is a peer ministry of brothers and sisters in the body of Christ. By sharing their own life stories, the team members invite hurting couples to see that the ordinary struggles of family life are invitations to holiness. Their examples of struggle, pain, and failure give others hope and help them to realize that other people are involved in the way they live their marriage and in their decision to stay married or not. After presenting Retrouvaille weekends for nine years I still feel excited about this much needed help for hurting marriages.

Who Comes to Retrouvaille?

Who participates in the Retrouvaille program? Couples of all ages, years of marriage, and economic status. A cross section of all married couples takes part. I remember a woman married six months talking about how hard those months had been and how much they wanted help to improve their marriage. Another man, separated from his wife for one year, expressed anguish because his town of 20,000 people had three parishes with programs for the separated and divorced but nothing for hurting couples. On Sunday morning of the weekend he announced excitedly: "My wife agreed to get back together this morning and we would like to invite all of you to our fiftieth wedding anniversary next year."

When Bonnie and Henry arrived on Friday night, she tried to convince us that their thirty-nine years together had been wonderful. On Sunday, she cried her eyes out as she shared how their eleven children had intervened, insisting that they participate in Retrouvaille by giving them the cost of the weekend as their Christmas present.

She added that she couldn't wait to get back home, 250 miles away, to give each of their children a big hug for saving her marriage. She showed no sign of any need to cover up her feelings.

On Friday night of the weekend, these couples look like any other couples in the community. You can't tell that many are separated, some divorced, and all have been living on the edge of desperation for some time. They don't have warts on their noses or knives in their hands. They may turn their backs on each other occasionally because of the pain, but they also hold each other's hand sometimes. What they have in common is a desire to save their marriage, or at least to look at the feasibility of trying to rebuild their marriage. Sometimes one spouse wonders why the other feels their marriage needs help. Many have been referred by counselors, who believe that Retrouvaille will help them heal their relationships. Others express disappointment because counselors either suggested they divorce or did not seem able to help them.

Most people in marital trouble don't want a divorce but don't know where to turn for help. Trapped in the misery stage of a relationship, they feel no hope, blame each other for the pain, and fail to see each other because pain has made them turn in on themselves. Some fight a lot, while others hardly communicate.

Some spouses carry scars from an unhappy childhood which make it difficult to relate in marriage. They may never have had a stable relationship, but thought that because they were in love, marriage would solve all the difficulties. Some carry unexpressed anger, others carry guilt, shame, fear, or insecurity, while still others have repressed their feelings. Some couples watched a fairly stable relationship deteriorate through busyness at work, alcoholism, infidelity, physical abuse, or drifting apart.

Relationship Building

Retrouvaille team couples try to avoid the role of counselors. Couples are asked to leave their problems and issues behind for the weekend and focus on getting to know each other better. If they try to solve problems, they will likely get hung up on issues that have previously frustrated them. This will distract them from the purpose of Retrouvaille, which is to build a stronger relationship. Once they have a good relationship, couples can usually solve their problems or reach out together to someone who can help them. Counselors are much more effective when the couple has a good relationship and can approach the issues with a learning attitude rather than a defensive one.

Ian MacDonald, who presents Retrouvaille on Prince Edward Island, comments: "Many professional counselors are forced by circumstances to focus on problems. That approach tends to be abstract and impersonal. We in Retrouvaille have the privilege of focusing on persons and feelings. That makes a great difference."

Mutual discovery and opening to relationship can happen in the safe setting provided by Retrouvaille. When both partners are willing to lower their defenses, they can begin to connect and develop intimacy. They can become themselves. We don't love people for what they should be or for what they accomplish, but for who they are. Partners who have experienced intimacy will not stay at that level, but having experienced it they will be more willing to work through difficult times. They come to realize that their own fears and insecurities create the limits and problems in the relationship. They make a primary commitment to overcoming these fears and insecurities and to exploring the conflicts until personal insight and resolution occur. Such openness may seem frightening, but a secure relationship depends on it. As they strive to understand rather than change each other, spouses can promote each other's growth rather than limit it.

When spouses can open their lives in this way with each other, they grow beyond fears and self-protection to enjoy a strong couple relationship. If they open up to God in each other's presence, admitting their weaknesses and needs, they discover even more about each other. This experience of new life in their marriage helps them achieve intimacy.

Greg and Kae were separated for months, both in individual counseling, and desperate for tools to put their lives back together. "At the time Kae brought the Retrouvaille weekend to my attention, I felt there was nothing that could guide us back onto the same path," recalls Greg. "At first I was resistant because I felt pressured by the immediacy of it all. I said yes, but with the agreement that I could leave if I felt it was pointless or too one-sided. A weekend together was pretty scary to think about after months of pain and conflict. We were making a choice to be vulnerable again and to give our marriage one more try."

"We found that the very walls we had put up to protect ourselves from feeling the pain also kept us from seeing and hearing each other, from touching and responding to each other, from experiencing each other's love," Greg says about the weekend. "I encountered every emotion I had ever known and realized how much I had let the relationship slide. I also realized how much work it would take to rebuild. I wasn't about to do it alone."

"Prior to the weekend we were focused only on ourselves and our selfish needs that emphatically were not being met," adds Kae. "Retrouvaille helped us become sensitive to each other again. Our focus slowly widened to include our spouse, and the way we talked began to shift from 'me' to 'we.'"

The degree of disappointment, hurt, deterioration, and despair in hurting marriages can't be healed in one weekend. Damage to a marriage occurs over an extended period of time; likewise the restoration process needs time. Couples are always marrying or unmarrying. "The weekend was a time to look at each other in a new way—a new beginning," recalls Greg. "The follow-up never seemed easy. We took it one session at a time because we still could not see three months down the road. There were growing pains in reaching out past my comfort zone to possibly grow in a positive way with Kae. We continue that process daily with the decision to love, even when we may not feel like it."

Kae's recollection of the months after the weekend is similar. "In the six months following Retrouvaille, I began to see in reality what I had been believing only with the eyes of faith. Greg and I are closer and more loving each day as we continue to use the tools we received during the Retrouvaille weekend and the follow-up sessions. The follow-ups were good for me. Each time Greg said he would go to the next session, it was another yes for our relationship. We gained support from other couples and I learned we were not the only ones with 'trouble in paradise.' I felt relieved not to have to pretend that everything was wonderful when we were still struggling. The follow-ups kept us on track and gave us building blocks for a strong relationship."

Greg and Kae found hope. "In our experience, we had a strong desire to put our marriage back together and the courage to do the work it would take. The Spirit begins to move in extraordinary ways with those ingredients plus the willingness to turn toward each other and to take a new look. Retrouvaille is *not* a magic quick fix, but the 'magic' in our relationship appeared when we worked at it. We pray and are confident that it can happen for others too." Another grateful husband wrote: "Retrouvaille hasn't eliminated all our problems or concerns, but it has given us the tools to work with. We've gained back our own self-respect. And our children have changed from being distraught and desperate to being happy and loving and enjoying life."

Sheri sums it up this way: "Wally and I never experienced anything else like Retrouvaille. Never have we communicated and shared and cried and forgave as we did then. I know not to expect a total change overnight, but this is the first time we've both been this optimistic."

Where Else Can Couples Turn for Help?

Retrouvaille supports counselors and works closely with them. They are not competitors, but friends who work toward a common goal of strengthening marital relationships. Many referrals for the weekend come from counselors, and most Retrouvaille communities not only encourage counseling but have identified counselors willing to help. A California counselor who sends many clients to Retrouvaille says that he saves six months counseling with the average couple.

Couples usually come to a counselor in a state of confusion and anxiety, often angry with and blaming each other. They have often identified the issue they blame for their difficulties. They expect counselors to be problem-solvers. But finding the solution to one problem is not likely to put the marriage back together. Fix one and another will come along. I compare this to looking at a butterfly under a microscope. You may see only a small part of the wing and be deceived into thinking this is what a butterfly looks like. Someone who listens to a couple's problems sees only a very small part of the relationship.

Couples have lots of strengths and weaknesses, healthy and unhealthy behaviors, that all contribute to the relationship. They need to look at more than the issues that cause them the most pain at the moment. Otherwise, they see themselves and their marriage mainly in the light of these problems rather than looking at the whole of their relationship. Retrouvaille has the advantage of touching on many aspects of a couple's relationship, and some of these areas are likely to be healthy rather than problematic.

Counselors do save many couples from the trauma of divorce. Wise help depends upon selecting a good counselor, then helping that person know all the facts. The divorce courts are full of couples who went for help and ended up with the recommendation they get a divorce. I hear couples on every Retrouvaille weekend share how a counselor gave them unwelcome advice to split.

In choosing a counselor, you have every right to ask lots of questions before beginning, or to ask for a preliminary interview before making any commitment. Simple criteria are enough to make the choice. What success has the counselor had in helping hurting couples? Do they use group therapy? Do you feel safe with this person or group? What spiritual values support the counselor's views?

When seeking marital counseling, you might look for a therapist whose primary area of expertise is marital therapy, not individual therapy, so you have a counselor well versed in the complexities of a love relationship. You will do best to find a marital therapist who will work with both spouses together. If you see different therapists, or the same therapist at different times, you can end up focusing on issues that help you live autonomously rather than harmoniously as a couple. When couples see a therapist together, they will discover more clearly how their personal issues affect the relationship, and both personal and relationship issues can be resolved together.

Resources other than private counseling are also available to many hurting couples. Catholic Charities agencies in most dioceses provide a variety of counseling services and support groups for couples in need. Church sponsored groups, such as the Christian Family Movement and Teams of Our Lady, provide support groups for couples seeking to build strong marriages. In many cities, groups of lawyers concerned about the divorce industry have organized a mediation service to work with both parties toward a wise solution of marital difficulties.

Twelve Step groups based on the original insights of Alcoholics Anonymous gather folks experienced in the same problem to share their experience and hope with one another. Hearing what has worked for someone who has been in the same situation provides a strong stimulus for change. Most of us can benefit by participating in a support group of some kind.

The Twelve Steps are a deceptively simple program for recovery. The program has three elements essential to making changes in our lives. First we need to recognize that our life is intolerable as is, making change necessary. Second we need to decide what to do to implement change. Third, we take the action that will bring about change.

The steps are the basic tools of the program. The first three are belief steps, the last nine are action steps. The program calls us to recognize that we cannot solve our problems alone; to recognize that an outside force (a higher power) can help us; to admit our problems and character defects to ourselves and confess them to another person; to make restitution for our wrongdoing whenever possible; to monitor our thoughts and behavior on an ongoing basis; to continue seeking spiritual assistance in dealing with our problems; and to let other people who need the same kind of help know about the program.

WESOM (We Saved Our Marriage) is one support group that utilizes the Twelve Steps of Alcoholics Anonymous for couples who have known the pain of adultery and want to heal their marriages. Although our society often suggests a spouse should divorce the unfaithful member, many wisely choose reconciliation over splitting.

Many Retrouvaille communities also include a Twelve Step family program as part of Continuing Our Retrouvaille Experience. While the Twelve Step approach focuses on the individual rather than the couple relationship, it provides a forum for exchange among people attempting to deal with marital problems. The group's purpose is not to solve individual problems but to provide support as members resolve their own difficulties. At meetings, people share struggles in their marriage relationship, what actions they took to help themselves, and how they are handling problems today by using the Twelve Steps. Practicing the Twelve Steps means that people have to take personal stock of themselves and be open to change.

Recovery is a process, not a cure that can be accomplished and forgotten. Relapses are inevitable. The Twelve Step program tells us that progress rather than perfection is what counts. People easily get discouraged when they fall back into the same behavior patterns. Support groups help us forgive and nurture ourselves as we seek healthier behavior. The Twelve Steps also offer a spirituality much needed by couples seeking reconciliation and healing. Few people can forgive others and themselves without God's help.

In this chapter we have looked at Retrouvaille, counseling, and support groups as sources of hope for marriages in trouble. The decision of where to turn is an important one. But even more basic is the willingness to consider that there may still be hope for your marriage. There's not much support for this option today, in a society where divorce is presented as the "quick fix" for a hurting marriage. In the next chapter we'll look at where you can find support for your commitment to marriage.

Reflection: Do we focus more on our problems than on our relationship as a couple?

Sharing: Do I feel hope or despair when I think about the possibility of saving our marriage?

2

"Who Supports This Couple in Marriage?"

Where does a couple turn when they face marital difficulties? Awareness of the problem is the first step toward change. But particular stresses and problems still stand in the way of intimacy. Powerful negative feelings have built over years. Resentments over a spouse's actions, hurtful behaviors, and emotional unavailability have accumulated for a long time. Couples who have been together for many years have deeply entrenched patterns of relating to one another. Even if both are willing to change, old patterns are difficult to alter and often the negative feelings remain even after the behavior has changed.

Moreover, couples in troubled marriages find it hard to find anyone who will support them in their marriage. Our society today has created a climate for divorce. In some circles it seems more acceptable to have gone through a divorce than to be confined to one marriage for life. Not only is adultery seen as part of the sexual freedom gained in the '60s, but people are even featured on TV talk shows because of their infidelity.

People tell me again and again, "You wouldn't believe how many people encouraged us to get a divorce when we were hurting." The common assumption is that people who suffer over an extended period of time in an unhappy marriage would do better to get out. Often, thinking that they're helping those who are struggling, friends, co-workers, and acquaintances try to support one spouse by running down the other.

While an angry person in the misery stage may be eager to hear reasons for the pain and isolation he or she is feeling, this kind of support from others only keeps the person stuck in an unhealthy phase of the relationship. Derision of a spouse hints that the relationship is no good, that the problems are all due to the other spouse's failings, and that the solution is out of this person's hands.

When people are hurting, the "liberation" of divorce looks attractive. But the kind of support these well-meaning people give only helps to postpone any solutions to the underlying problems in the relationship.

Too many people are ready to welcome others to the world of marital breakup because it justifies their own struggles. Irene, facing an unwanted divorce, complained that several support groups she tried encouraged her and other recently separated people to proceed with divorce rather than consider reconciliation. People at the same precarious point in life can form a dependent bond that perpetuates a situation of avoiding solutions.

While divorced friends may draw a couple further toward divorce through commiseration, married friends may suddenly take on a new role with a hurting couple as protector, guardian, or parent. Hurting couples may threaten their relationship, so they come up with all the reasons their marriage flourishes while someone else's is in difficulty. In the process, they point out how wrong the hurting couple have been in their relationship, hinting that they themselves are superior. This merely increases a couple's feelings of failure and inferiority.

Another obstacle to finding support is that couples themselves often think it is no one else's business whether they marry, how they live their marriage, and whether they stay married or not. Yet, many people, including children, families of origin, neighbors, and employers are affected by the way a couple lives their marriage and by their marital breakup. Family problems and the breakup of marriages rank as the highest cost to employers and the most expensive social problem of our day.

Sometimes couples find it too difficult to talk about their problems. When their relationship is in shambles they pretend everything is fine until one person moves out and they can't hide the truth anymore. They hide the reality of a hurting marriage and keep at a distance from those around them because they want to belong and fear rejection.

"Traditionally," says Joan Hoxsey, a family life director, "couples don't talk about the intimate details of their marriage with anybody, sometimes not even with each other, but especially not with other folks. They can talk about things like the house or the car, but not about values and issues of friendship. Couples need the support of other couples to know that what they are going through is probably not too different from the experience of others in general."[1]

Studies show that couples who have a strong support system have a better than average rate of survival in marriage. They turn to relatives, friends, groups, and community as valuable supports in dealing with stress. Couples friendly with seven or eight other couples strong-

ly committed to marriage have a much better chance of
marital success.

Structured support groups provide a network of
friends that can supplement or make up for the absence of
an extended family. Particularly in a mobile society like
ours, couples may live hundreds or even thousands of
miles from their extended families. Sometimes when
couples are trying to make a decision about such issues as
children or handling conflict, getting input from other
couples can give them much-needed insight and objec-
tivity.

The greatest source of support often comes from
other couples who may or may not realize the great ministry they're performing. When I asked Ken and Vicki to
get involved in ministry to the engaged, Ken said, "I don't
know why you're asking us. I don't think we are different
from other couples. If it hadn't been for my sister and her
husband, we would never have made it through our first
year of marriage."

"What did they do for you?" I asked.

"Every time we were hurting or in trouble, they
would get together with us to talk."

The Church as a Family of Families

Studies of who survives in marriage today show that
the strongest factor is the faith life of the couple; the only
other significant factor is a strong support group. Research
into well-functioning families consistently shows that
church membership and the maintenance of the family's
spiritual traditions and rituals are a source of strength for
family life. Church membership often provides the basic
network of support so essential to families. Mobile
families, for example, often find the new parish provides
the pool from which friends, interest groups, baby sitters,

sympathetic professionals, and advice on schools are drawn.

Families are asking the church for help in this time of family instability. They want the church to affirm the value of marriage and family, to support family life, to counsel in times of family difficulties, to help with the pressures that afflict the family today, to provide moral leadership, to share compassion with the broken, and to call families to serve others.

In 1987, U.S. bishops asked American Catholics where they most find God in their lives. Most said they found God in their marriages and in their family life. When the bishops asked where people most needed help from the church, the overwhelming response was "in my marriage and family life."

Because many people have close links with the church at the key transition points of the family cycle, especially birth, marriage, and death, churches have access to families in a unique way. The church is the only institution with the whole family as its client, which gives it a special role in family care and ministry.

While many churches may say that couples are sacred signs of God's love, too often we expect them to ride off into the sunset after their wedding to live happily ever after without our help. We attend weddings as observers rather than as people making a commitment to support and challenge this new couple. Weddings have become the personal show of the couple rather than a communal celebration of support that continues long after the wedding day.

For this reason, the U.S. bishops created a comprehensive plan for family ministry in 1978. They called for ministry to families in various stages, including the engaged, newly married, parents, hurting marriages, and the separated, divorced, and widowed. In the decade of the '80s, however, when this plan was to dominate the ministry efforts of the Catholic church in the United States, little gain was made on ministry to hurting marriages. In fact, the only family ministry making major strides focused on the separated and divorced.

The question is whether or not we are serious about the care of marriage. Marriage is badly battered in today's society. Pope John Paul II reminds us: "The modern Christian family is often tempted to be discouraged and distressed at the growth of its difficulties; it is an eminent form of love to give it back its reasons for confidence in itself, in the riches it possesses by nature and grace, and in the mission which God has entrusted to it."[2]

Unfortunately many hurting couples are not actively involved in church. Some are indifferent, but more are alienated by hurts, or caught in pain for which they are so angry at God that they have pulled away. They often expect the church to be judgmental, as was the rules-oriented church of their youth. Now that they are failing to live up to these expectations for marriage, they feel they are not "good" members of their faith denomination.

This may be an area where programs such as Retrouvaille can reach out to couples in a special way. Arlene deliberately married civilly because of her anger with the Catholic church. She participated in an alienated Catholics support group for seven years. Interviewed after a Retrouvaille weekend, Arlene said: "This is the first time that I have experienced a church that cared." She added that she "was really impressed by the fact the church was getting involved with people and their hurt and pain. I don't know if it is the church's responsibility to reach out to families in crisis, but that is my expectation."

Dolores shares how she experienced a caring church when she participated in a Retrouvaille weekend: "I thought back and felt this is what God wanted for the church: a priest who would be a father to listen to their cries and to lift them up again when they fall, brush their knees, give them a warm hug, and tell them they are loved before they send them on their way."

John also found a caring church: "This past weekend may have saved more than our marriage. I have not been a very devout Christian these past few years, and this weekend has given me reason to evaluate my faith. I believe I was touched more on a personal level because I had a change of heart spiritually."

Much of the spiritual growth in our generation has happened through Cursillo, Marriage Encounter, Parish Renewal, and other programs with sufficient time for a conversion experience bringing us back in touch with the Lord. Married couple and family retreats can help people rediscover each other and renew their commitment. Many churches sponsor a series of conferences or sharing sessions for couples focused on deepening relationships, understanding families of origin, couple spirituality, conflict resolution, or other helpful topics. Such programs can all offer couples a sense of support for their marriage and family life.

What Can Hurting Folks Offer Others?

Many of the most successful enrichment programs offered through the church are presented by peer ministers. Couples who have learned through their experiences are valuable resources. Although we think of hurting couples as needy themselves, I find that getting them involved in helping others often enables healing. The happiest people I know are those who give of themselves rather than getting caught up in their personal difficulties.

Chris and Mary Ann note that, when they got married, others advised them to spend their early years just focused on each other. "It was a lonely hell. We were lucky, because we were married only a year when we made a Marriage Encounter weekend. The message there was to share our lives with others, and that has made all the difference."

Many couples who get involved in serving others find themselves part of a support community sharing in a specific ministry. Tom and Vivien know that by sharing their frailties and strengths, their joys and sorrows, they are channels of God's healing and peace:

> The Lord has allowed the healing in our lives to be an empowering hope for other couples to allow forgiveness and healing to take place in their lives. Our pain has been turned into gift for others. Through sharing the healing of the hurt and pain we put each other through we can give others hope that they too can begin again and take responsibility for their own relationship. Healing and forgiveness can take place in their lives. They can make that same leap from desolation and emptiness, anger and frustration to healing, wholeness, and new life.
>
> We do not have the perfect marriage. We can laugh now but we must remember that once we cried. We have to continue to work on all areas of our relationship if we want to grow. We do not have all the answers. But we do have hope and we are willing to use our own imperfections and woundedness as a tool to help each other and other couples.[3]

Family ministry is based on certain assumptions. One is that all families, no matter how hurting or fragmented, have tremendous strengths and the power to help and support other families. Another is that individuals and families who have been through a certain experience have a quality of caring and support to offer others in a similar situation that is unique and healing. The real experts in marriage and family ministry are spouses and family members. There are times when specialized, professional help is needed, but the basic ministry to families lies in the day to day support that family members and peers give to each other.

Ministry is a response to those in need. Married couples experience a vulnerability that makes them people in need of support, encouragement, and nurturing. Wanda and Terry's story is typical of a hurting marriage: "We went to three marriage counselors and a priest for help with our marriage. Each one told us that our problem was communication, but no one helped us learn how to communicate. Instead, they all suggested that we separate. We didn't want to separate, and we already knew we couldn't communicate, but we couldn't learn how on our own."

People struggle a lot with the question of where and how to see God in their lives. We see God wherever people are in need and cry out for our help. Family ministers have gained their own awareness of God, often in the midst of struggle, and can now point to God's presence in hurting relationships where the couple is blind to anything beyond their own problems. Peer ministers help others see the face of a loving God when nothing but darkness seems to be present.

Tom and Vivien reflect that experience:

> We have certainly received more for our own relationship than we have ever given. Yet through the years and the hundreds of couples we have presented weekends to we never cease to be awed, humbled, and amazed at the healing and beauty that God's love can bring out of so much hurt and pain. You just realize you know there was no way that whatever you said could have brought about that much change in anyone. You know that the healing power of Jesus' love is present and active through the power of prayer.[4]

Affirming a Love Story

Perhaps one of the most powerful supports for those struggling to make their marriages work can come from

the lived witness of those who have persevered and discovered the enduring love of a lasting marriage.

Ina Hughs wrote an editorial in the *Detroit Free Press*
called "Dance of the Dinosaurs."

> "Are you married?" asked the young woman cutting my
> hair.
>
> "Yes" I said. ". . . it'll be 22 years."
>
> She stopped snipping and looked at me as if I were a
> dinosaur. "Aw, come on," she said wide-eyed. "To the
> same person!"
>
> I guess we are kind of like dinosaurs, he and I. If
> statistics keep heading in the direction they are going,
> we're apt to be extinct.[5]

In a throw-away society, "till death do us part"
means until we are tired of this relationship or until someone more attractive comes along. Advertisers make us ask
"What's in it for me?" assuring us that if we are unhappy
a new drink, a new car, a new job, or maybe even a new
spouse will make our life better. Why should we be unhappy when we only go around once here on earth?
Divorce insurance, pre-nuptial agreements, and no-fault
divorce all help prepare for the time we should move on
to someone else.

We badly need "dinosaurs" to make us believers and
serve as symbols of hope today. A lifetime is a long time
to be married, especially now that we live so much longer.
Like heroes in other areas of life, stable marriages provide
a model, convincing us that permanence is possible, and
that Jesus wasn't fooling when he asked us not to put aside
what God has brought together.

In the midst of our broken world, talk shows and
magazines pay more attention to failed marriages than to
couples who succeed at love. Healthy marriages, which
tend to create healthy families, need to be affirmed and
celebrated as models for us. While many couples drown

from indifference, rejection, and loneliness in marriage, "dinosaurs" remind us another alternative is possible.

I would like to share one of my favorite love stories with you. Bill and Alma farmed in northern Minnesota. Alma was nominated for State Mother of the Year by the American Legion Auxiliary. When the governor honored the nominees at a banquet in St. Paul, Alma was named a Merit Mother or runner-up.

When Alma returned to her hometown, the folks thought they ought to celebrate one who had made good. They scheduled a potluck supper at the Legion Hall and filled it with townsfolk and farmers. After they enjoyed a meal together, someone decided that they should ask a few persons to speak.

Alma's students from the days she came to that area to teach and married a local farmer shared how she had affected their lives. The mayor shared what she had done for the community, usually in projects with Bill. The pastor talked about all the years she served as chairperson of the Ladies' Guild, taught religious education, and cleaned the church. Finally the master of ceremonies asked Bill if he had anything to say. Bill got up, smiled at their friends, said "Didn't I make a good woman out of her?" and sat back down.

Although he was joking, Bill's comment reflected truth. You never saw Bill leave the farmhouse to go out to do chores or go to town without taking time to visit with Alma in the kitchen, showing his affection by giving her a kiss, a hug, or a waltz around the kitchen. When he got back from town or the fields, before getting busy with his chores, Bill would again take time to stop in the kitchen for a visit and show of affection.

Often Bill and Alma went for a walk on the farm, perhaps returning with Alma carrying a bouquet of wildflowers he picked for her, while he sang a love song in his Irish tenor voice. They raised nine children in this setting. After eight of their own, they adopted a six-year-old girl who had been in thirty foster homes and was badly scarred. With her insecurity she tested them often, but today is a mother herself and the president of a state barbers' association.

Although Bill's health was poor in later years, Alma died first. On the morning after her funeral, Bill was eating breakfast with some of his children when he started to cry and exclaimed, "I really have to thank God for answering my prayers."

"What prayers, Dad?" I asked.

"For the fifty-four plus years that your mother and I were married, I prayed daily to live longer than her. I never wanted her to be alone," he commented.

I wanted to ask if my mother knew about this prayer, but it didn't seem appropriate at that moment. Instead, my thoughts went immediately to a plaque they had for years, now hanging on the wall near the table, which quotes from 1 Corinthians 13. One sentence on that plaque reads, "Love is not self-seeking."

Reflection: What effects have the changing values regarding permanence and fidelity had for me?

Sharing: Who has supported us in the more difficult moments of marriage?

PART II

SELF-AWARENESS AND COMMUNICATION

3

Will the Real Me Please Appear?

Our self-image has a profound effect on relationships. When I don't like myself, I don't expect another person to like me either. So I try to be acceptable by presenting someone other than the real me. Most of us don't like ourselves very well. What I bring to this marriage is me, with my limitations and strengths. The more I know myself, and can share who I really am with another person, the more likely we can build an intimate relationship.

Most of us have put together a jigsaw puzzle. Suppose that we have a "calm before the storm" scene, with red roses, green grass, blue sky, and an ugly gray storm cloud rolling in. If I randomly pick out several pieces of the puzzle, getting only pieces of the gray storm cloud, I might think the puzzle is not very pretty.

We all tend to do this with the puzzle of who we are. We pick out a few pieces, not randomly of course, but because we are most aware of them. Usually we pick out pieces of our behavior that we don't like—failures, weaknesses, all those parts that make us self-conscious. We may even overlook the pieces that are red roses. For example, if I am patient most of the time but occasionally become impatient, I am not likely to see myself as a patient person.

Unless we can see the whole puzzle, recognizing both the gray and the colorful pieces as part of the whole picture, we easily get into trouble. Many people don't like themselves very well. Consequently, they don't expect others to like them either, and they act accordingly.

If I expect that another person will see into me and not like me, I am not anxious to share myself. I use protective behaviors to hide the real me or to reveal only that part of myself that I expect another will accept. Often we over-emphasize a part of our personality that seems acceptable to others and makes us appear strong. People have predominant personality types, which can be expressed by a variety of masks.

For example, the Achiever wants to see results, likes solving new problems, likes variety and action, gets impatient with routine details, and doesn't always take others' interests into account. The Achiever may develop the mask of the Perfect Parent, the Good Provider, the Quarterback, the Bulldozer, Superman, or Supermom.

The Logical Thinker doesn't readily show emotions, is uncomfortable dealing with others' feelings, likes to analyze and put things in order, and can stand firm against other people's ideas or arguments. The Logical Thinker could become the Controlling Person, the Analyst, the Intellectual, Mother Superior, or Mr. Right.

The Friendly Helper tends to be very aware of other people and their feelings, likes to please others, lets decisions be influenced by other people's wishes, dislikes telling others unpleasant messages, and is sympathetic. The Friendly Helper dons the mask of the Nice Guy, the Good Listener, the Clown, the Martyr, Mother Hen, or Community Volunteer.

These masks are the way we act with others to be accepted and to feel good about ourselves. They are the ways we function in life. These masks aren't phony disguises. Rather, we use them to cover up a poor self-image. When we exaggerate these personality traits, though, they irritate others and keep us from relating openly and honestly with those around us. Moreover, through our masks, we set standards for ourselves that are impossible to live up to. Our failure to achieve these goals reinforces our poor self-image.

For example, my personality type is the Friendly Helper. I wear the mask of the Nice Guy. I want my efforts to please others so they will accept me. I do for others, listen to others, care about others. I don't readily expose feelings that don't seem "nice," nor do I easily acknowledge my failures. The more I don't feel good about myself, the more I need others to see me as good. I will inconvenience myself to help others, ignoring my own needs and priorities to please others.

How We Got That Way

I frequently ask couples, "What did you learn about marriage from your parents? Do you want to pass these lessons on to your children?" Family behavior and attitudes are transmitted from generation to generation. We see ourselves through our parents' eyes, get our belief about self from our parents, and then tend to repeat our family history. If our family life was unhealthy, we learned destructive behavior from our parents and will pass it on to our children unless we break the cycle through change.

We begin to learn early in life how to get what we want and how to hide from others. Our family of origin is a school for life. Whether our families function in healthy or unhealthy ways, are strict or lenient, have lots of secrets or are open, have members highly dependent on each other or independent, will determine something of our behavior. Other experiences, such as coming from a large family, growing up in a single parent home, or finding it difficult to achieve success in school or sports can result in our need to get attention in other ways.

Children in unhealthy families lose their true self and bring family baggage into the marital relationship. A lot of our present behavior and issues, which seem to be caused by present circumstances, actually derive their power from our childhood. Our responses and our feelings reflect our earlier self-doubt and sensitivities. Conflicts are easier to work through when both spouses understand the extra-sensitive issues and their origins. For example, if one partner innocently comments about the other's appearance and gets a response of hurt or anger that seems out of proportion to the comment, it may well be because of childhood feelings of being unattractive or overweight.

We get our core belief about ourself from our parents. If parents are abusive or shaming, a child's inner identity is destroyed. Frequently, our shame came from our parents' failure to show emotions or to affirm our feelings, using us to meet their emotional needs, forcing us to hide secrets of shame, failing to be present to us, or abusing us sexually, physically, or emotionally. Children conclude that the abandonment or abuse is their fault, that they were bad and so deserved such treatment.

To compensate for abandonment, children develop their own survival behaviors. They project a false self that distracts them from the pain and loneliness of their true self. Ultimately they lose contact with who they really are.

In many families, shame governs every family member. They hide from themselves and others, afraid of their true selves and alone. They learn to be silent rather than express their pain. Their life is spent reacting to the person who controls family behavior. When their identity lies outside of themselves in another family member, and they react to that person rather than being themselves, they are left powerless and spiritually bankrupt.

Adult Children of Alcoholics and other groups stress the importance of looking back into our childhood. If we can review our childhood in order to understand rather than to blame, then we can move forward. In doing this, many people experience a great deal of anger at their parents. We need to remember that our parents usually did the best they could with their own limitations. One of the tasks of building a healthy self-awareness is to forgive those who have harmed us.

Behaviors learned in childhood are often repeated because they work, protecting us from fears that have haunted us since childhood. Our protective responses were fixed in us long before we met our spouse. When we perceive the connection between present behavior and past experiences, we can begin to move beyond behavior that was appropriate and necessary in childhood but may no longer be needed. We can begin to change our behavior to be more appropriate to our present situation. Learning to recognize and eventually change protective behavior that makes us critical, closed, or manipulative is a key to better relationships.

A child's self-esteem comes from approval by significant people who make them feel lovable or worthy. At times approval and love get confused. Children, and perhaps their parents, carry a mistaken idea that disapproval means they're not loved. As children, we were approved when we did what was "right," like saying please and thank you, being well mannered at the table, and quiet when adults were talking. We got approval for achievements such as talking early, behaving well in class, and getting good grades in school. When we did not behave according to the values of our parents and other significant adults, we got disapproval through such signs as the silent treatment, scoldings, irritated looks, or threats of physical punishment.

Our self-doubts began very early in life as our feelings met disapproval. If we were not approved for ourselves and our feelings, we began to mistrust the rightness of the feelings themselves. We began to look outside ourselves for the right way to be or feel, hoping to avoid rejection. The more we gave up trusting our own inner experience, the more we became vulnerable to being controlled.

When we feel disapproval, we often show sadness or cry. If parents are not in touch with their own feelings, they have a hard time acknowledging their child's pain or the possibility they have hurt the child's feelings. They attempt to stop the expression of pain by comments such as "Big boys don't cry"; "Come on, now, don't be such a baby"; "Don't be so sensitive"; "That's nothing to make such a big deal about"; or "Stop crying, or I'll give you something to cry about." Eventually children learn to shut off the pain so they won't be unlovable. As children grow up, they see their difficulties in life as further proof they are wrong or inadequate.

Healthy Self-Love

In marriage, a lot of separation comes from one or both spouses pulling away from the other because they don't feel good about themselves. We may use self-protective or manipulative behavior while blaming the other for our pain. An old axiom says: "I can't love another until I first love myself."

Joan Hoxsey, a family life director, comments: "I am

becoming more and more convinced that you can't have a healthy relationship without feeling good about yourself individually. We couples have to find out who the 'I' is before we become 'We.' You might think that people accomplish this at age twenty-five or thirty, but it's a lifelong process."[6]

If we don't love ourselves, we find it difficult to love others. We also find it difficult to believe that anyone else can love us. We can't accept the fact that someone who can see us as we really are will still truly love us. We test others, asking them to prove that we are lovable and telling them all the reasons why we are not lovable. I can only allow another to love me without conditions when I truly love *myself* as I am.

Self-knowledge and self-love are essential to healthy relationships. We can only love others for who they are, and we can only be loved for who we are. Such openness may seem frightening, but security in a relationship depends on it. As couples strive to understand each other, they can promote each other's growth.

Some years ago, two California psychologists developed the Johari Window theory, which I find helpful in understanding how we build or diminish relationships. They drew a window with four squares. One square represents the area of self commonly known by me and by others. For example, others may know as well as I that I like to read and have a definite concern for marriage and family life. A second square represents the area known by me alone. I know that I sometimes struggle with fears of failure, yet I hide this from others. A third square represents an area known only by others. I don't think of myself as shy, but others have told me a number of times that I am shy. The fourth square is that which is unknown by me and by others. I don't know whether I would be codependent if married to an alcoholic because I have not experienced this.

The size of each of these squares varies from time to time. When I have good communication, the area of knowledge common to me and others expands as I share more about myself and listen as others point out what they observe about me. The more the window of common knowledge is opened, the more I am at ease with myself and my relationships. When I have poor communication or feel insecure and untrusting, the window of common knowledge becomes smaller.

If someone has hurt me, I may close the window of common knowledge by refusing to share anything personal about myself. Sometimes this window is closed because I am suppressing past experiences, such as painful experiences from my childhood. Because I am not open to hearing what others might share with me, I lose a mirror by which to view myself. The more threatened I am, the more I distort the information I share with others and the more distorted my perception of what they reveal to me. When I have closed the window of common knowledge, or peek only through a tiny opening, I pull away from others and live in misery.

Often the most deceiving window is that of self-knowledge. I may think that I have a fairly good self-image, without realizing how much I cover up. I may be unwilling to look at my shadow side. What I see as junk, such as the brokenness in my life, others may see as a gift for compassion, healing, and strength. We don't easily open the window to self-knowledge because we're afraid of seeming incompetent, weak, or unworthy of others' love. Expectations that I should be perfect, fear of disappointing others when they know me, and the false security of sharing my masks rather than my real self keep me from total openness. Yet my reluctance to reveal myself also keeps others from knowing my good qualities, dreams, values, needs, and convictions.

The fourth and unknown area is not totally unknown

and unknowable. It is not unknown to God. Often it is not beyond my understanding if I approach life with a will to learn and to grow. I can come to know this area better through prayer, asking God to help me confront my dividedness, or listening as God reveals more to me through a spouse or in the depths of my heart. I am also able to learn more about myself when I open up to the risks of self-discovery.

When I don't want to open the window to the unknown, it may be because I approach God with guilt rather than belief in God's unconditional love for me. I may have a mistaken belief that God expects me to be perfect. To overcome this, I need to know that God loves me as someone who has areas of brokenness as well as areas of health and strength.

If I have a hard outer shell, I deflect the love God and others have for me, and fail to experience their love, forgiveness, healing touch, and desire for relationship. To be completely open to self and to others, to knowing and being known, in a sense to become real, is to awaken to joy. Then I am at peace with myself.

When spouses can share their lives in this way with each other, being open and honest, they grow beyond fears and self-protection to enjoy a strong couple relationship. If they are open to God in each other's presence, admitting their weaknesses and needs, they discover more about each other and experience new life in their marriage. They are able to achieve intimacy and community.

One of the greatest barriers to self-knowledge and openness with others is the inability to forgive ourselves. If I don't forgive myself when I've done wrong, I can't take the next step of reaching out again to God and others. This forgiveness is as important as the forgiveness I seek from God or from others.

If I simply try to forget what happened, it lingers until I've dealt with it and been healed. Sometimes I pretend the fault is not that serious when deep down inside I know it is. Or I try to avoid responsibility for my actions by blaming someone else. Taking responsibility for my faults, though, is more than saying "That's the way I am and I can't help it." I have to truly face my faults and make a sincere effort to change.

Forgiveness does not mean that I will never make the same mistake again. Nor does it give me license to keep falling back into the same pattern of behavior. When I forgive myself, I turn from staring at my faults to looking forward with hope of doing better.

Hope for the Future

Those whose self-image and self-acceptance is controlled by the family they grew up in can recover their true self by getting in touch with their feelings, changing their protective behavior, and forgiving themselves and other family members who hurt them.

We need to go back in our memory to understand who we are. We don't go back to blame but to let go of the past so we can get on with life. If we don't deal with our family of origin, we keep repeating the same behavior. We might look at such questions as:

◆ What were the family messages (For example, "You're as good as your work!" or "But you're a girl")? How do they still control my choices and behavior?"
◆ What were the family rules I followed?
◆ What made me acceptable?
◆ What made me feel bad or weak?
◆ What did I do to protect myself?

Sharing these experiences with another can be very helpful. They help with insights and support. When we share our sorrows, the burden is lightened, and when we share our joys, the joy increases. Sharing helps us develop trust. Judy believed that sharing her childhood experiences of incest with her daughter would mean that she would never see her daughter and granddaughter again. Instead, sharing these painful memories deepened their mutual understanding of the years when her daughter was growing up and strengthened their present relationship.

After participating in Retrouvaille, Carol wrote: "Thank you for helping me understand what free will is. I've always been so heavily laden with 'should's' and guilt. Now I see how that has hampered my attitude toward God, my husband, and society in general. I know I have a long way to go for a full understanding, but for the first time in my life it feels okay to be me—loved, honored, and accepted by God . . ."

Reflection: What are the qualities I want others to see in me and what do I need to feel good about myself?

Sharing: What protective behaviors can I recognize in myself that keep me from getting closer to my spouse?

4

"I Never Knew You Felt That Way!"

Through working in a hospital, I have been privileged to help with several conferences on Traditional Indian Medicine. Basic to their medicine is a belief that our physical, emotional, intellectual, social, and spiritual life all need to be intact for a person to be healthy. If any one of these are not healthy, then the whole person is unhealthy or "dis-eased."

People of our generation pay a lot of attention to their intellectual life and their physical life. More recently, we have learned to care for our spiritual life. But we haven't paid as much attention to our emotional life yet. These parts are not distinct from each other but are all a part of who we are. If we neglect to care for any one part, then we are less than we could be. To be more whole, we need to pay better attention to our emotional lives.

Most of us have a difficult time identifying our emotions, let alone communicating them to someone else. An emotion is a spontaneous inner reaction to a person, place, or situation, or an energy that is instantaneously released inside of us. It is a feeling that I have when I come into contact with something outside myself, or even with a thought that I have. For example, I enjoy whitewater canoeing, with the warm wind splashing water across my face as I steer the canoe through the rocky rapids. My emotional reaction is one of excitement and contentment.

Very often we confuse feelings with thoughts. When I can use the words "I think" in place of "I feel" and the sentence makes sense, I have expressed a thought and not a feeling. When I can replace the words "I feel" with "I am" and it still makes sense, I am likely expressing a feeling. I might say, "I *feel* that women should have equal opportunity with men," but I have expressed a thought. I should say, "I *think* that women should have equal opportunity." Phrases such as "I feel that" or "I think that" or "I judge that" express a judgment.

Our feelings constantly change and vary in intensity. I can have many feelings at once. My feelings are a very large part of who I am at a given time. If I don't look deeply enough into my feelings, I often use adjectives to name my feelings. When someone asks me how I feel, I tell them "I feel okay" or "I feel good." These words do not name feelings.

Often, we name surface feelings that mask deeper, stronger, more vulnerable emotions. For example, anger may mask fear and insecurity. It seems unacceptable to feel insecure or vulnerable so we don't go beyond safe, surface emotions or we become unemotional.

Our emotional life has many layers. Under each layer of feeling lies another. Eventually we get to the heart of our feelings and find there a deep need. If our needs are fulfilled, we experience pleasant feelings; if our needs are

unfulfilled, we experience unpleasant feelings. In revealing our feelings, it is very important to share our positive
and affirming feelings as well as our unpleasant or negative feelings.

To understand ourselves, we need to be open to and
accept all our emotional reactions. We need to understand
that no other person can cause or be responsible for our
emotions. We like to blame others for our emotions. For
example, we might say, "You make me so mad." But no
one can make us feel anything. They can only stimulate
the emotions that are in us. When we stop blaming others
for our emotions, our feelings can provide an important
learning experience. Why are we so angry? Something was
already in us, waiting to be activated. Getting in touch
with our emotions will help us get in touch with ourselves.

Most people have no idea what causes their feelings.
Protective feelings always come from our beliefs. We don't
choose to feel depressed, angry, or scared, but we have
chosen the beliefs that create these feelings. For example,
if I feel scared, it's probably because I believe that I'm being
threatened in some way. If I feel emotionally hurt, it is
because of my beliefs rather than someone else's actions.
We need to accept the reality that we cannot be emotionally hurt by another person.

In the same way, we can only be responsible for what
we do, not for how others feel in reaction to what we do.
Our feelings and responses always arise from our own
values, beliefs, fears, and expectations. Therefore it is impossible to be responsible for another's reactions.

Emotions summarize and express our highly individual and unique human experiences. They reflect the
security or insecurity of our childhood. One reason we
have difficulty expressing our feelings comes from very
early training that some feelings are okay and others are
not. When we tell young boys that big boys aren't afraid
or don't cry and nice boys don't get angry, they are likely

to feel ashamed of their feelings and forced to repress them. When we laugh at little girls when they express their feelings, implying that emotional wimpiness is a quality of women, we stop them from taking more risks.

Churches often give the message that "good Christians" are always nice, caring, even-tempered, never angry, and always long-suffering. To fit this image, we would have to deny our humanity and be basically dishonest. No one is without anger or always even-tempered.

Our families, too, train us in expressing or repressing feelings. Some families readily express hostility and anger, but fail to express tenderness, love, and appreciation. Other families appear to have unwritten rules that allow the expression of kindness, concern, and positive feelings, but then suppress irritation, shame, self-doubt, and expressions of disagreement or dislike.

In many ways we imply that some feelings are acceptable and others are not, that some are good and others are bad. In reality, all emotions are okay, neither good nor bad. Because we have no control over our feelings, they are neither right nor wrong. Some are pleasant, while others are unpleasant. When people use adjectives such as good or bad to describe their feelings, they are actually describing the actions that are a response to their feelings. What we do as a result of how we feel can be good or bad because we can control our actions.

Communication and Relationships

In rebuilding broken or damaged relationships, we often need to learn to express ourselves through our feelings. In that way we give the real gift of ourselves to another. We become transparent to one another. Sharing your feelings will allow your spouse to know you in a new way, while also allowing you to know yourself in a new way. If you don't open up and share your feelings, your spouse may project his or her feelings onto you. If you tell someone about conflict in your relationship without describing vividly how you react emotionally in a conflict situation, the listener will assume that you react the same way as he or she does, and that is not so.

A negative or inaccurate reaction says, "You don't have a right to your feelings," and shuts down our willingness to risk. When a husband tells his wife she shouldn't feel lonely even though he cannot communicate at a feeling level, or she tells him he shouldn't feel scared or inadequate on the job, it's because they're not willing to let others be themselves. When one marriage partner takes a risk and is belittled or receives no response at all, another layer of protection builds around feelings.

Even when we discount a partner's feelings with motives springing from love, we deny another's right to feelings. This keeps them from understanding themselves better. For example, a wife may discount her husband's fear of inadequacy on the job because she sees him as the competent person he is and because she hopes that if she minimizes his feelings he will no longer harbor them.

Every emotional reaction tells us something about ourselves. If we want to know something of ourselves, our self-image, our needs, and our values, we need to listen very carefully to our emotions. Too often, we repress our emotions out of fear of rejection or for fear these emotional reactions will be used against us. Repressed feelings have a way of coming out in self-destructive ways. We need to share these emotions with others, and then they usually are no longer a threat to us.

When I share my feelings with you, I am in some ways sharing my whole life, giving you the ultimate revelation of where I have been and who I am. When I confide my feelings of loneliness, fears, doubts, shame, and joys with you, I let you get to know the real me. I tend to project an image of strength to others. When I can open up and reveal my fears, my joys, and my hurts, other people become more aware of who I really am and realize they do not know me as well as they or I supposed.

The most common fear we have is to be found out and rejected. We even fear admitting our deepest feelings to ourselves because we're afraid of losing self-respect. It is much easier to talk about problems than to expose a feeling, because with feelings we give others a glimpse of our real selves. When we reveal ourselves through our feelings, we trust ourselves to another's understanding and acceptance. Often we find it much easier to stay busy with activities than to share how we really feel about ourselves, about one another, and about our lives together.

In healthy relationships, spouses can dare to risk sharing feelings and the other responds to that risk, not by discounting the feelings but by responding to them. They may say, "I know how you feel, because I feel that way at times too." Rather than discount the other's feelings, they share their own in a reassuring and supportive way.

Encouraging people to express their feelings does not give them license to take out their emotions on another or to blame others for their feelings. We can tell others we feel angry, but hurling abusive words at another because we are angry is not a valid expression of the emotion. If we try to manipulate others by attempting to make them feel guilty for having caused the feelings or to force them to give us the sympathy we want, we're being unfair. If we ventilate our feelings in such a way that we feel better but the other feels worse, we have not shared our feelings appropriately. The only valid reason for sharing our feelings is to communicate with others in such a way that they can know us better and we can have a more intimate relationship.

Couples seeking to deepen their relationship will discover that being more open with their feelings can be of great help. A good way to start is by sharing on the question, "How do I feel when . . .?" Some areas for this sharing might include:

    . . . when you seem to be rejecting my feelings?
    . . . when you seem annoyed with me?
    . . . when I think you are acting superior in our relation-
        ship?
    . . . when I don't seem able to reach you?
    . . . when you interrupt me?
    . . . when you say no to my requests?
    . . . when something else seems more important to you
        than I do?
    . . . when you praise and compliment me?
    . . . when you make a sacrifice for me?
    . . . when you ask me to help you?
    . . . when you tell me you love me?
    . . . when I tell you I love you?

Be creative as you think of areas of your relationship to explore with each other.

Reflection: How do I feel when someone blames me for their feelings?

Sharing: How were feelings shared and accepted in my family and how does that affect the way I communicate feelings?

5

"He Never Talks to Me!"

Steve and Carol were separated for four months after a four year marriage and three children. Carol took the children back to her parents' home. Steve's mother called to ask if I would talk to the couple if Carol came back to Minnesota. Once both were at my office, I asked Carol how she felt four months earlier when she left home. "It was the hardest thing I have ever done in my life. I thought I was a total failure." Carol continued to share her feelings of disappointment, hurt, and failure.

When she stopped talking, I asked Steve if he knew Carol felt that way. "No," he answered, "I thought she couldn't wait to get out of there with what she was saying." Then I asked Steve how he felt that day. "We were having a terrible fight, and I felt relief when Carol slammed the door. But she wasn't in the car yet when I wanted her back." When I asked Carol if Steve had communicated this feeling to her, she said he had not. In two hours that day, we were able to make plans for Carol to return home, and for the couple to get help rebuilding their relationship.

Communication difficulties are common to all of us. Counselors quickly realize that they are talking to two good and well-meaning persons who give each other only garbled messages, or who are so guarded they communicate very little. This creates the situation in which a wife finally asks her husband: "Honey, do you love me?" She is usually disappointed by his answer: "Of course I do. I married you, didn't I?" This old joke reflects the reality of far too many marriages.

The Associated Press polled divorce lawyers in 1988 about the causes of divorce.[7] Lawyers saw communication problems, either lack of communication or the inability to communicate, as the biggest cause of divorce. The only other major cause, they thought, was couples drifting apart. Money, sex, in-laws, and children were at best minor causes, and they saw infidelity as a symptom rather than a cause.

Communication is vital in a marriage relationship. Couples who have a stable marriage list communication as a major satisfaction. Couples with marriages in distress usually list poor communication as the major problem area.

Yale University studied couple communication and had so much difficulty believing the results that they tried three different methods with three diverse samples of married couples. They discovered that the average couple spends only two minutes a day or fourteen minutes per week in communication. Moreover, in that time they communicate information rather than deeper feelings, needs, and values.

Dolores Curran describes the life of many couples: "Life becomes notes on the kitchen table where people just pass one another. There is no time to talk together, to deal with the marital relationship. Then, when the stress gets too high, they increase the emotional distance and become more polite. They don't have to face the fact they are not seeing each other or are too tired to talk. Then, after a while, they become only roommates."[8] Communication patterns are learned, not inborn, and most of us are poorly trained. Many parents don't provide a good model of couple communication for their children. Often, the hectic pace of modern life limits the time available for good communication.

Learning good communication skills can improve any marriage and can help a couple work through misunderstandings and difficulties. An important skill to learn is the ability to make "I" statements. Because both what we say and how we say it are essential parts of effective communication, "I" and "you" words make a big difference. "You" statements try to direct and control what is happening as we focus on the other person. "You" statements frequently come across as nagging, blaming, or attacking, especially when accompanied by a pointing finger or strong emotions in the speaker's voice. They provoke defensiveness and counterattack in the listener. "You" statements can leave scars and diminish trust, seriously damaging a marriage relationship.

"I" statements express our own feelings, thoughts, needs, and views. "I" statements allow the self-disclosure and openness that lead to understanding. Even in moments of anger, "I" statements allow feelings and viewpoints to be expressed without blaming or attacking the other person. When we share our inner feelings or needs, we make ourselves vulnerable, but we also invite understanding and create a climate of acceptance and trust.

Openness in Communication

Communication needs real openness, which demands trust, risk, and acceptance. Openness means that I believe in my goodness and accept myself with my strengths and weaknesses. I'm willing to let you really know me, and I trust that you will accept me. I become vulnerable to you, taking the risk of sharing what might seem foolish or weak. Openness requires a decision to trust, so that I am willing to share the person I really am, rather than the person you want me to be, or the person I want you to see. If I reveal one of my inadequacies and you immediately try to change me, I am likely to close up again. I want to be accepted as I am. Openness also needs good listening skills, in which I try to know the other person and to accept that person as he or she is.

Good communication involves self-awareness. Healthy people know who they are as individuals, and take responsibility for their own feelings, perceptions, and desires, while not taking responsibility for others' feelings, perceptions, and desires. They communicate honestly with each other. Unhealthy people fail to be aware of their feelings or they repress them. They disassociate from their feelings and often respond with silence, angry judgments, or rage.

Communication is both verbal and nonverbal. We communicate by being silent and by inaction as well as by talking and by action. We need to listen to nonverbal communication. Body language expresses my feelings at the moment, even if I don't admit them verbally. For example, a firm jaw says I'm uptight or angry, a slumped body and shoulders indicate I'm depressed, pacing back and forth tells you I'm anxious, and a big hug says I'm happy to see you or maybe that I need the security you offer. Whether I look into your eyes or avoid them, the way

I hold your hand, and the look on my face can tell you a lot about our relationship.

Body language is often the way we know another's feelings. I ask a teenager, "Did you do it?" He denies it, but his head hanging down, his eyes avoiding contact, and his bodily posture tells me he feels guilty. Body language is like a barometer of feelings. We need to check it frequently to be certain we understand correctly. When inconsistency between words and body language occurs, a nonverbal message is heard.

Communication can help us to keep things in perspective. Often we set impossible standards for ourselves and others. When we can't meet them, we feel as if we have failed or we blame others for being imperfect. Learning to laugh at ourselves and our unrealistic expectations reminds us that we are neither superpersons nor failures, but human beings doing their best to live and love in healthy ways.

One hears very little laughter from hurting couples, which is a tragedy, because humor and tears often provide a very helpful release for tensions. A sense of humor can help hurting couples keep things in perspective, so they don't feel trapped by the drudgery, misery, and conflict. Laughter can diffuse the failure and blame. There is increasing evidence that laughter can be therapeutic. People who laugh experience less stress, because laughter helps to diffuse potentially stressful situations and release tensions. Healthy laughter causes physical relaxation, reverses stress, and rids us of hypertension.

Dialogue

Learning to communicate well is certainly one of the most important skills we can acquire. To achieve successful communication, we need a strong desire or motivation. We also need a commitment to persevere, even when our efforts seem to meet with failure. As in acquiring any skill, failures will happen. Too often, the setbacks discourage us and we turn away from our commitment to communicate with our spouse.

Commitment to communication, like any commitment, is a matter of priorities. You might ask yourself: Am I willing to give time to communication? Am I willing to be known and to know another? What fears do I have about sharing myself honestly with another?

One of the most effective ways to communicate is through writing and sharing these writings, a method called "dialogue." I often ask couples struggling with their communication to write letters to each other and then to share based on these letters.

Writing can be a very effective way to get into our feelings, our needs, and what we should communicate before we start to talk to each other. Without this preparation, it's easy to get defensive or to stop listening because we are trying to formulate our responses. Writing gives us time to be aware of our innermost thoughts and feelings and to put these down so that we can be sure of what we want to say. We have time to reflect without someone interrupting, challenging, or giving advice.

We write to help the other understand us. We can't presume that person understands unless we have communicated very well and openly. Often, when someone says, "I didn't know you felt that way," we realize that we haven't taken time to look at how we really felt either.

Spouses read each other's writing to understand, not to change each other. Trying to change another's feelings, or telling someone not to feel that way, contributes to the other person's fear and weakness. What I write is a gift of who I am to the other person. If the recipient tells me I shouldn't feel as I do, that person is bashing my feelings. When the other accepts my feelings, no matter how irrational they may seem, he or she helps me learn what is behind my feelings.

After spouses have read each other's reflections carefully, they explore each one's strongest feeling together. They help each other to discover what is going on inside. This is a learning experience. Giving this attention to each other, especially by communicating feelings and not simply information, opens a couple to intimacy.

Dialogue is not a time for solving problems, but for understanding each other so a relationship can grow deeper. Listening is the key to dialogue, because it moves us beyond discussion to the kind of understanding everyone longs for.

Another technique I have found helpful with couples in counseling is asking them to set aside an hour once or twice a week for communication. Taking a few minutes to think about what they want to share before the exercise begins is good preparation. During the hour, each will get thirty minutes to talk while the spouse gives the gift of listening. The one talking can talk only about himself or herself, not about the other person or their relationship. The listener can't make comments, but is simply trying to understand. After each has had thirty minutes to share what they believe most important, the exercise is finished and not to be talked about further.

Communicating at the feeling level, something most of us don't do very well, is especially important for any marriage that has experienced a breakdown. Good communication could have helped Roger and Sue, who divorced after two years of marriage. Already in the divorce process when I saw them, Roger complained that Sue was "always bitching at me." She thought he was the coldest person she had ever met.

As we explored the reasons for their statements, Roger admitted that he stayed away from home as long as possible after work each day because he didn't want to face Sue. He would stop at the local tavern until after the regular supper hour. It soon was apparent that Sue's "bitching" was really begging.

She came from a warm Polish family that showed affection, while Roger's Norwegian family expressed very little physical affection. He was uncomfortable with her need. Also, they lived in a trailer home next to his parents' house on the farm, and Roger, the eldest, was not about to show affection in front of the brothers and sisters who were usually around the trailer home. When I asked Roger whether he had ever seen his father kiss his mother, he easily said "No!" Then he smiled and said, "I guess he must have. They have fifteen children."

Reflection: What areas am I still afraid to talk about with my spouse? Why?

Sharing: Am I aware of how I use nonverbal communication, such as rolling my eyes or crossing my arms, to communicate how I feel?

6

What Did You Just Say?

An old adage says: "You can't do two things if one of them is listening." Yet most of the listening in marriage competes with the distraction of children, phone calls, television, bills, household chores, and all that comprises home life. Typically, we half-listen, preoccupied with our thoughts rather than hearing and feeling what another is saying.

Most parents know from talking to their children how easy it is to hear lots of words without enough concentration to hear the message behind the words. We frequently ask, "What did you just say?" and hear in response, "Why don't you listen?" Often we feel miles apart, frustrated and irritated because we can't get through to each other.

Loneliness and alienation are very painful when we want to know and understand another person. When we want to control the other person, often because of our fears, we can use all kinds of nonverbal signals such as yawning, looking at our watch, making faces, raising our eyebrows, or changing the volume and pitch of our voices. These take away the other person's freedom of self-expression, as they convey a judgment rather than the desire to know that person.

Listening, according to Webster's Dictionary, means "paying close attention to another." I am personally present to you when I give you all my attention. Good listening is an active effort that makes use of ears, eyes, and emotions. It takes energy and concentration. It also takes putting aside our own agenda while trying to identify the thoughts and feelings of another person.

There are times when I listen with my head only, so I understand the message but I miss the emotional undertones. When a teenager says to me, "I don't want to go to the dance!" I might hear lack of interest when he is really telling me that he doesn't think anyone cares or he feels lonely with his peer group. He really needs me to hear the deeper message. Listening tells others we care about them.

When I ask someone to listen to me, I want that person to enter my world and understand who I really am. When someone listening to me seems bored or distracted, I hardly want to risk a deep sharing of myself. When the listener gives signs of closing me out, impatience, or disappointment, my inner fears and insecurity drive me back to self-protection. When I sense that another understands me and knows what it is like to be me, I no longer feel alone but reassured and energized.

Most of us quickly slip from the listener's role when we interrupt another as they start to reveal themselves. We feel a compulsive urge to advise them, supporting our advice with experiences of our own. No doubt we think of listening as getting the facts so that we can solve the problem, but advising blocks communication.

A popular reading called "Listening" starts:

When I ask you to listen and you start giving advice,
You have not done what I asked.
When I ask you to listen to me and you begin to tell
    me why I shouldn't feel that way,
You are trampling on my feelings.
When I ask you to listen to me and you feel you have
    to do something to solve my problem,
You have failed me, strange as that may seem.
Listen! All I asked of you was that you listen, not to
    talk or do—just hear me.

John Powell writes in *Happiness Is an Inside Job:* "Most of us listen only long enough to shoot from the lip—to offer a little advice, tell an anecdote from the past, narrate a few stories of our own experiences. Sometimes we cast ourselves in the role of problem solvers." The key to good listening, Powell says, is a "patient curiosity that wants to know what it is really like to be you."[9]

When I actively listen to another person with my heart, I help that person discover herself and open up to sharing her feelings and needs. Others do the same for me. Often I am not in touch with my own feelings because I haven't focused clearly on them. Sharing these feelings with another helps me to clarify them. It's like having another help me put the pieces of a jigsaw puzzle together so that I can see the beautiful picture they create.

Listening means I open myself to the uniqueness and mystery of the other without judging that person's intention or motivation. Being open challenges me to accept what is going on inside the other person, even though the feelings are different from my own, without judging what the other person is experiencing.

Couples and families with good communication listen even to routine questions like "How are you?" or

"How was your day?" with their eyes and hearts as well as their ears. They pick up the body language and emotional tones, and ask questions that will clarify. People in healthy relationships respond to feelings as well as words, and they respond in such a way that we feel deeply understood.

Listening Is an Art

Listening is an art, and like any skill it must be practiced and perfected over time. We can begin to improve our listening by choosing a good time to communicate, uncluttering our minds from distractions, using eye contact, reading body language, or repeating what the other is saying to be certain we understand and to let our partner know we are listening. Good listening is the first step toward good communication. One man acknowledged that learning to listen with his whole being was "an intimidating experience."

Learning to dialogue and not merely discuss is one way to learn to listen. Dialogue deals with feelings, while discussion deals with content. In dialogue we do not have an agenda nor are we trying to accomplish anything useful. One does not seek to dominate the other nor are we trying to negotiate. We are trying to know each other, not to convince or persuade each other.

Communication based on sharing of thoughts, ideas, and values is called discussion, which means analyzing different points of view rationally and objectively. Dialogue involves a sharing of feelings and emotions. It comes from two words: *logos* meaning "the word" and *dia*, which means "through." Dialogue implies a stream of meaning flowing between us, emerging as some new creative understanding. This shared meaning is the glue that binds our relationship together.

Dialogue demands an atmosphere of trust and openness. Marital communication breaks down most often in the absence of sharing feelings. Communication of information is necessary in marriage, but dialogue holds the relationship together and forms the bond that facilitates discussion. Dialogue creates a sensitivity to what is going on in the relationship. We become more than a couple solving problems. We achieve an energy that can be called communion.

In dialogue, partners make a gift of themselves to each other when they communicate. Communication tends to be superficial without this deeper level where we discover who we are. We need to know more than another's ideas or values for good communication.

In healthy communication we listen and respond. This response becomes possible when we can get into the other person's feelings and show empathy. For example, a wife who listens to her husband's fear of losing his job, recognizes his fear as legitimate, and identifies with it is responding. If she tells him just to work harder, she is reacting. Her unrealistic demand that he change the situation comes from a projection of her own fear that he will be out of work. Often we react because we're not enough in touch with our own feelings to be objective about the other's feelings.

One obstacle to empathy is that we think much faster than we speak. Consequently, the listener has to work at concentrating on the one sharing or the mind takes little side trips. When this happens, the other person may well notice it and conclude that the listener is bored or indifferent.

The invitation to empathy begins with the question of what it is like to be the person sharing. When someone tries to go beyond hearing what we are saying to understanding us—how we perceive ourselves and life, and all the dimensions of what we are sharing—the message is that they care.

A good listener seeks to know the uniqueness and mystery of the other person, to enter into new discoveries of what it's like to be that person. He or she tries to get rid of expectations of the other by being totally open to that person's sharing.

Fifty percent of success in communication is determined by how well we listen. When we are threatened or disinterested, we don't listen very well. Listening is part of the decision to love, since we love only that which we understand.

Very often spouses in counseling seem to be on different wavelengths or so expecting they know what the other will share that they never hear what is said. I spend a lot of time trying to get spouses tuned in to each other or interpreting what I think I heard someone say. Using dialogue as a tool, couples can do this for each other. I know of nothing that can help couples learn healthy communication as well.

Healthy families know how to communicate, both verbally and nonverbally. They use and recognize signs, symbols, body language, smiles, and other physical gestures which express their feelings of caring and love. They deal with silence and withdrawal in a positive, open way. Communication doesn't mean only talking and listening, but all the clues to a person's feelings. Spouses don't have to say "I'm hurting" or "I am in need." A quick glance tells each other that. They respond without words in ways that indicate empathy and love, whether or not they resolve the pain or needs.

Reflection: Do I sense my spouse listens to me? How do I feel about this?

Sharing: People who care enough to listen communicate their interest and faith in us. How well do I listen to verbal and nonverbal messages?

PART III

*R*ELATIONSHIPS

7

Why All This Misery?

A story that I think says a lot about marriage centers around a husband who liked women with long legs. Whenever he and his wife went for a walk, this man would be all eyes if a woman with long legs went by. One day when this happened, his wife blew up: "I just can't stand this. Every time you see a girl with long legs, you are all eyes watching her instead of me. If you ever do that to me again, I am going to leave you!" A properly repentant husband promised not to let his eyes stray again.

The next time they went for a walk and a woman with long legs came by, his eyes strayed again. His wife began to cry, saying: "How do you think I feel when you look at all those girls with long legs and here I am just five feet two? If you like girls with long legs so much, why didn't you marry one of them?"

"Honey," he said, "I thought you'd change!"

Obviously, this story is not about long legs, but about her shopping habits or housekeeping, and about his television habits or sports. We have expectations that get in the way of seeing who the other truly is. We have preconceived notions of what we want in a spouse long before we meet that person. We also have definite expectations of ourselves and the role we will play in marriage.

We meet someone, fall in love, and marry. Our romance probably obscured the hopes and expectations we had. Perhaps we believed that such a wonderful person would fulfill all these expectations and that we would happily meet each other's needs forever. In the romance stage, we find a real excitement in this person we believe was meant just for us. Any free moment means a chance to be together, or on the phone with each other. Couples in the romance stage have high expectations and lots of dreams. They can't believe the love that seems so strong now will ever be questioned, even though they see the pain of many other couples. The falling-in-love experience gives them the illusion that marriage will solve all their difficulties. But this is only the first stage in any relationship.

Most divorces occur at one of three vulnerable periods in marriage, each a major time of disillusionment. The first three years of marriage, when our unrealistic dreams are shattered by the reality of our own and our spouse's limitations, is the most likely time for divorces.

The "seven year itch," when we have achieved our initial dreams of two careers, two children, and our own home, and now find ourselves in a rut, creates another dangerous time, whether it's seven or ten or twelve years down the road.

The third major time of divorce centers around the "empty nest time," when the youngest child gets into the teen years and no longer depends as much on parents. Couples who have invested much of their lives in their children look across the table at each other in this stage and wonder if they want to spend the next thirty years together.

Stages in a Marital Relationship

Psychologists tell us that every relationship goes through four stages: romance, disillusionment, misery, and awakening to joy. These stages occur over and over again, unless we get stuck in the misery stage and don't know how to get beyond it.

In the romance stage, we focus on the other person. No one in the world matches our friend. In disillusionment, we are bugged by the traits or behavior of the other and begin to focus on ourself. In misery, we become totally turned in on self and, if we notice the other person at all, we believe that person is the cause of our pain. The focus in the awakening to joy stage centers on us as a couple as we experience unity once again.

In the disillusionment stage, we grow disappointed with ourself, our spouse who doesn't always make us happy, and our marriage. Barbra Streisand points to disillusionment when she sings: "You don't send me flowers anymore." Romanticized expectations give way to truth. Little things begin to be annoying. It is not the toothpaste squeezed in the middle, the dirty socks left on the floor, the mood swings, hair curlers, and burned dinners that hurt so much. It's the judgment we make that we are not special to this person if he or she isn't careful with the toothpaste or the socks. Our vision of ourself and our spouse gets distorted.

This is a time when our expectations begin to give way to reality. A woman may realize that she cannot keep the house as clean as she had once envisioned. A man may realize that his dreams for a successful career are not ing through promotions or other job oppor-

ve become more absorbed in our own feelings of failure, we react by lashing out and expressing a projected disappointment with our spouse more often. She nags him for not sharing the housework or taking time for household repairs. He misses the affirmation she gave him in their dating days and may accuse her of pushing him to be successful.

Marriage doesn't seem as exciting as what they dreamed of while dating. Both may feel burdened with responsibilities, finding little time for talking let alone lovemaking. Fights or silence replace the deep conversations and understanding of previous years.

Slowly, unconsciously, behavior changes, and spouses begin to live a more self-centered relationship. Couples gradually develop what Marriage Encounter calls a "married singles" lifestyle. Gradually they begin thinking more of their own interests than of their partner's. They think they might be happier pursuing individual goals and aren't anxious to do things together or spend time together.

What is destructive about the married singles lifestyle is not what we do, but that we use sports, television, newspapers, work, or clubs to avoid each other and to avoid the difficulty of the marriage relationship. Now the club we joined innocently becomes a frequent activity to keep us away from home, a way to show our spouse who is boss, or a way to be in control. The paperwork a spouse brings home from the office begins to say "My work is more important than you."

We may sincerely believe that fulfilling our own personal dreams will be best for us in marriage, but that begins a vicious cycle of even more independent decisions and behaviors. After a while, we are trying so hard to survive personally that we can hardly survive together.

Joyce and Pat were separated at one time but are now back together. Joyce explains:

> Perhaps the most important thing to notice about these married singles activities is the mentality or attitudes behind them. What often happens is that we do these things to escape. If we're not getting strokes at home, we go get them someplace else. This lifestyle becomes destructive when we look elsewhere to get the compliments and good feelings we used to get from each other.

Pat's insights are similar:

> This married singles lifestyle creeps into our lives like a thief in the night and burrows into our day-to-day existence so thoroughly that we simply accept it. We say: "That's the way our marriage is—that's the way other marriages are—so it must be normal." But the moment when we accept it as normal is the moment when the dream we had for our marriage begins to die. . . . Underlying all our justification is the fact that if we ever once admit that the responsibility is ours and not society's, we will have to change the behavior that once led us into trouble in the first place. And *that* is really what we fear the most.

Misery is actually the bottoming out of the disillusionment stage. Feelings of bitterness, distrust, anger, hopelessness, and being trapped take over. Spouses find it hard to protect themselves from getting hurt again. They get hung up on the issues or problems they experience at the moment, because their relationship is not healthy and strong enough to work through these problems. They find many good reasons not to change and they blame each other for their pain. They fail to see each other because the pain has drawn them into themselves.

Usually we get trapped in the misery stage because we don't like ourselves. We put up all kinds of protective barriers, turning in on ourselves as we hide behind these walls. Art and Jeanne's story is typical:

> The rug was pulled out from under us when I, Jeanne, went through a trying pregnancy, after which the baby died. I had a low self-esteem and came to believe I wasn't a good mother. Why else would God let my baby die? Soon after this I, Art, began having problems at work. I began to question my value as a provider. I developed a very poor self-image.
>
> Because we didn't see value in ourselves as individuals, we lashed out at one another and blamed each other. Our home turned into a battlefield every night. There didn't seem to be a way out. We were killing each other with our criticism and our arguing. Even as it was happening we couldn't believe it. We were supposed to be one of those "good Christian couples"![10]

Couples often come to counselors at this stage, expecting a cure from the pain of their difficulties. If the counselor simply helps them solve their problem with finances, sex, or children, they will soon stumble over another issue.

In the hopelessness of the misery stage, people often give up. "I made my bed, now I have to sleep in it!" "It's a living hell, but what can I do?" No light shows at the end of the tunnel. The spouse doesn't seem understanding or even present. Spouses frequently sleep in separate beds, talk to one another only when one of the children has a problem, or communicate only through bitter arguments. Divorce seems to be the logical way out.

Most divorced people never wanted to separate from their spouses. They just didn't know how to handle the problems and the pain. Tom and Vivien's story is typical:

> The daily joys and struggles of caring for our family, a sick child, and numerous runs to the emergency room took some of the focus off our own shaky relationship. Our life together became a compounding of big and

little insensitivities over the years when we were coexisting partners. Things didn't seem to be settled or talked out; it seemed whoever yelled the loudest caused the other to back down and after routine silences one of us would apologize about the reaction, but the situation was not generally looked at for fear of another argument so it was just added to the mountain of unshared feelings, hopes, frustrations, and resentments. It was just left to fester and erupt at a later time. We were crying and dying on the inside but to others we appeared to be quite the normal couple.[11]

Decision to Love

People who promised to love each other until death often renege on their commitment in the misery stage. Couples run off to the divorce courts without testing their creative ingenuity and resources. Love works, but we have to work at it. "People don't reconcile anymore," says Donald Hillstom, a Minneapolis lawyer who specializes in men's rights issues. "There's no religious or moral or ethical concept in our society to hold people together."[12]

We avoid getting stuck in the misery stage by making a decision to love. Love is not a feeling, although we identify some feelings as "love." Feelings change. Love is a decision and a commitment. If we can recognize misery for what it is, we can make the decision to love.

The person who makes a decision to love has made a commitment to be loving whether a loving feeling is present or not. If the feeling is there, so much the better, but the will and commitment to love is still exercised when it isn't. The common tendency to confuse love with the feeling of love lets us deceive ourselves. We easily profess love for our spouse or family, but it may be difficult to find evidence of that love in our actions.

The hardest time to make our life an act of love is during a period of pain, whether physical or emotional.

Pain magnetizes our attention and absorbs all our energies. We become very self-centered, thinking only of ourself. There is little energy left over for loving. But somehow
in the midst of that pain, we have to make a decision to
love almost in spite of ourselves.

I best understood "love is a decision" late one night.
I was at Sam and Della's home, talking about their marital
problems. The previous day I had spent three hours with
Sam and his employer, trying to save his job driving a
gasoline transport until he sobered up again. Now Della
had called me over to their house because their two high-
school-age sons had packed and were leaving home. Their
nineteen-year-old had already left home because of his
father's surliness when drinking. As we talked late into the
night about why Della stayed with Sam, and she explained
how painful marriage had been, she said: "Father, day
after day after day I have to decide to love Sam." She was
doing just that, despite the pain, despair, and misery. In
time, Sam got his life together. Because of Della's decision
to love, they hadn't lost their marriage, and they had the
opportunity to rediscover one another and their relationship.

The fourth stage in a marital relationship, called
awakening to joy, is a time of forgiveness, rebuilding,
making the needed changes and beginning again. We
strive again for unity. Love means asking what is the most
loving thing I can do for another rather than asking what's
in it for us. This may mean telling someone the truth they
do not want to hear or bringing up a discussion they want
to avoid. We offer what we think will help another to grow
or foster their uniqueness. We never force their response
of acceptance. This giving is the result of a committed,
thoughtful decision, and not simply a passing feeling.

We never reach the fourth stage and stay there.
Rather, we keep cycling through the stages of a relationship, unless we get stuck in the misery stage. Romance and

awakening are life stages in a relationship because we focus on the other person and on the relationship. Disillusionment and misery are death stages because we focus on self. Love means dying to self so that I can live for another. True joy comes not in the "poor me" or self-centered stages of a relationship, but in moments of unity and creativity.

Most people contemplating divorce are trapped deep in the misery stage. Instead of recognizing this, they blame their spouse for the marital difficulties. Most couples at this stage don't need someone to put a bandage on their hurts or to liberate them from their marriage; they need someone to help them discover that this lonely, living hell comes from being turned in on oneself in the misery stage. They need to know that the way out lies in making a decision to love.

At this vulnerable time, however, most couples hide their pain, pretend publicly that everything is normal, and think they are the only ones with such pain in their relationship. They are fortunate if they can find a support group of couples who can share the experience of misery from their own relationship and offer their own stories of having reconciled and built a stable marriage. This kind of witness can give others the hope needed to reach out again in love.

Reflection: When have there been deep feelings of isolation and loneliness for either or both of us in our marriage?

Sharing: Share a time when the decision to love your spouse has led to the experience of joy.

8

Who Is the Dirtiest Fighter?

Mike and Chris made a Retrouvaille weekend while divorced. In the open sharing at post-weekend sessions, Chris never spoke until near the end of the last session. Then she simply shared a puzzled insight: "We had never had a fight. But we were divorced!" Chris acknowledged that her efforts to avoid conflict and sweep disagreements under the rug had not worked.

People we care for and live with can stir two of our most intense emotions—love and anger. Indifference is a greater enemy of intimacy than conflict because it tells us we are not involved with one another. No involvement means no conflict, but it usually suggests that no love exists either.

Conflict is a necessary part of relationships if we are to solve the issues that face us. Conflict is a sign that the relationship is important. When people are involved with one another in a relationship they want very much, they will become aware of the differences that exist between them.

We laugh at the conflicts in marriage on television shows and movies because we recognize something familiar from our own experiences. It appears funny when it happens to someone else. But real conflict is no laughing matter because it makes us feel uneasy. As a result, most couples do not handle conflict well.

Defensive or Loving Behavior

Most of us react to conflict with protective behaviors, because we fear rejection, judgment, or another's anger or domination. In protective behavior, we blame the other for our feelings and behavior, denying that anything is wrong with us. Loving behavior, being open to learning from the conflict, is a healthy alternative. When we are willing to look at ourselves, seeking to understand why we feel the way we do and how our spouse feels, we can gain insights that lead to healthy change.

It is important to learn how and why we protect ourselves so we can become less protective and more loving. We instinctively protect ourselves from some real or imagined fear. The fear may come from past experiences such as being shamed or criticized. Our fears may have started in childhood when we received disapproval for being ourselves. A conflict now stirs up the fear that our spouse will find us unlovable or not okay.

We may react by going along with whatever our spouse wants. We do this not willingly but out of fear or guilt. For example, a wife may make love so her husband won't get angry. When we give in, we feel bad about ourselves and ultimately lose our identity.

Some people use anger to protect themselves. Anger is a normal human response. When a person feels threatened, frustrated, or attacked, the body automatically triggers a defensive reaction. Physical changes occur in our body and we feel an emotional surge of anger. Anger, like other unpleasant feelings, is not bad. But too often we use it in hurtful ways. Anger is a powerful source of energy. While it can be destructive, properly handled it can also be constructive. Couples face the challenge of learning how to handle anger so it becomes constructive rather than damaging to their relationship.

We learn how to handle anger through years of observation and experience with family, friends, television, and other events. We may learn to yell and scream, to call names, to blame, or to use threats. This often vents our anger. Venting clears the air as we say whatever comes to mind, often attacking or blaming others. Venters gain release from the pressure by expressing anger, even if it hurts others. Venting anger often causes hostility and leaves scars.

Others learn to suppress anger. They walk away, ignore, use the silent treatment, or find other ways of avoiding conflict. They seem unable to face a situation that might arouse strong negative feelings between them. Suppressors spend a lot of energy pretending everything is okay, trying to convince themselves and others that nothing is bothering them. This "peace at any price" mentality has the price tag of a superficial truce, a shallow relationship, and a build-up of resentments. The issue does not disappear. Often it festers until it can no longer be contained, and then it explodes in some fashion.

Both venting and suppressing anger can be harmful to a marriage. Neither works well in building a close relationship. Couples need to learn ways to handle anger that channel its energy into actions that make the relationship stronger. Couples can work together to break old patterns and develop more effective ways of handling anger. Conflict then may become a learning experience rather than a time of defensive behavior.

Couples sometimes use competition to solve conflict, choosing a power play that implies "I win, you lose" or a victim stance that says "You win, I lose." Neither position is healthy or helpful in a relationship. For example, one person tries to enforce his or her wishes at the expense of the other, or one sacrifices his or her concerns to satisfy the other.

When we focus all our energy on protecting ourselves, we end up going around in circles rather than solving conflicts. Both may try to control each other, which results in fights. When one tries to control and the other complies, we don't fight but we don't solve deeper issues either. When one spouse is indifferent, we each go our own way, avoiding fighting, intimacy, and growth. Protection always leads to negative consequences, such as poor self-esteem, feeling unloved, or power struggles. Spouses caught in these situations usually do not understand what is going on between them.

Conflict Resolution

Conflict resolution cannot take place until we first understand what conflict is. Conflict is the emotional tension that results from incompatible needs or values. We can have conflicts within ourselves. For example, we enjoy eating but we have to diet, or we want to spend an evening alone with our spouse but we realize the children need some time too.

Conflict is inevitable in a close, intimate relationship. To say that conflict is inevitable does not mean that there will be verbal and physical abuse; it means that differences exist that need to be solved, and these differences will often cause irritations leading to anger and conflict.

Two people bring together their individual backgrounds, values, habits, expectations, interests, and needs. When a couple lived separately, differences may have seemed minor. In intimate living, they become much more obvious. A characteristic that once seemed attractive may become irritating when experienced on a daily basis. Rose Marie says she married Jay because, contrary to her rigid father, he was so laid back. She feels very angry, now that they have teenage children, when Jay still holds back and leaves the discipline to her.

Conflict often happens when two people want different things at the same time. One spouse may want to go dancing while the other wants to stay home and watch television. Conflict may occur when things are not as we expected or as we want them to be. The night owl who marries a morning person and expects her to be alert and playful when he is ready for bed is likely to blame his wife for her seeming indifference. The introvert, who turns within to find answers, then just gives the spouse that answer, and who draws strength internally, gets frustrated by the extrovert who finds answers by talking issues out and who finds the source of energy in other people.

An old axiom says, "The dirtiest fighter is the one who refuses to fight at all." Someone who doesn't want to rock the boat, and skirts the issues to avoid conflict, ultimately damages the relationship. Fighting can actually get us through a conflict to a level of greater intimacy. The following rules can make fighting less painful. Spouses may want to post rules for fighting on their refrigerator door or bathroom mirror.

1. *Fight.*

2. *Fight fairly.* Remember that you are trying to grow together. Often we learned unhealthy or unfair ways of fighting from parents or from our culture. These make winning at any cost the most important thing. If one spouse wins, both lose.

3. *No name calling.* Calling a spouse a name such as "stupid" simply backs that person away from a fight. Do not call each other names except the affectionate ones you normally use, such as "Honey" or "Dear."

4. *No third parties.* The argument is between the two of you. Larry and Nan involved his mother in their fight and neither wants to face her now. She will likely remember the issue long after they have forgotten. Even counselors can stir up past hurts and failures.

5. *No past history.* If it's already been settled, don't bring it up again. It is irrelevant and merely a way to smear your partner. It's okay to go back to learn, but not to get something on your spouse.

6. *Stick to the subject.* Find the issue and don't bring in other issues just to prove your point. When he comes home late and she feels taken for granted or unloved, deal with feelings to make the real issue apparent.

7. *Don't hit below the belt.* Don't throw your partner's weaknesses in his or her face. You may win the argument but lose more than you gain. On the other hand, don't be too sensitive to what your spouse says.

8. *Don't go to bed angry.* Finish the fight. Dragging a fight out is as life-draining as avoiding a fight. Unresolved anger can destroy intimacy.

9. *Maintain a sense of humor.* Laughter is sometimes the best medicine. It's good to be able to laugh at yourselves, but don't laugh at or make fun of your spouse.

10. *Hold hands and/or look in each other's eyes.* Being in contact with each other, rather than turning your backs, is the hardest rule. However, it takes the focus from the issue and places it where it belongs, namely on the most important person in your life.

To begin to resolve conflict constructively we first need to understand each other's feelings. When we approach conflict with the intent to learn, we look primarily at our own behavior and feelings, and only secondarily at our spouse's behavior and feelings. The following five steps can help with this exploration.

1. Decide what the issue is and then dialogue about it. By dealing first with feelings in conflict situations, the real issue may become apparent. When he comes home late for dinner and a fight ensues, it's not his coming home late, but her judgment that he is being inconsiderate. She may feel taken for granted or insecure in his love. These underlying feelings elicit a strong emotional response to a seemingly small matter. Decide what and whose the issue is, and where and when to talk about it.

2. Write your feelings. Stick to feelings and try to develop them fully. This invites a lot of learning about yourself as well as the other person. Exploration may be painful, but when we go inside ourselves to understand feelings of rejection, disapproval, or shame, we heal the pain that now affects our present relationship. We need to be willing to feel pain in order to enter into learning rather than self-protection.

3. What are your thoughts and what assumptions are you making? Sometimes a conflict can be settled by each partner understanding the other's original intentions and feelings in the incident. Important reasons usually exist for any behavior. We can learn a lot by listening to each other and confronting our fears. In exploration, we look for reasons for what we are doing. We can ask questions such as "Where did we learn our protective behaviors?" and "What values, expectations, and fears do we operate from?" For example, I may have an unspoken assumption that says if you loved me, you would never come home late, forget my birthday, or leave your clothes lying on the floor because it upsets me.

4. What do you see yourself doing? How are you acting or reacting to these thoughts, feelings, and assumptions? What have you chosen to do or not to do? Methods

used to resolve differences vary with the flexibility and creativity of the couple. Whatever the method, each partner must feel that his or her point of view and preferences have been considered before the resolution of a conflict is considered successful.

We need to look at how we talk about this issue. We usually want to talk about the issues rather than how we deal with the issues. Exploration calls us to get down to the level of feelings, especially the fears that motivate our actions. We need to ask a number of questions. Why did we get angry rather than sharing our deeper feelings? Why and how do we protect ourselves and what happens when we use protective behavior? What are the negative consequences when we get angry?

5. The next step is to look at whether we are willing to change. Are we willing to open our feelings more fully to our spouse? What can we do differently to resolve this? Do we have other options? What can we do for the sake of the relationship? Sometimes we can compromise, where each gives up something and each gains something. One partner may give in to what the other wants as a gift to the other or because the issue is not that important, although it's unhealthy if the same partner always gives in. We may agree to disagree at this time because the differences are so great or because each partner feels so strongly that we don't see any other solution.

Unresolved anger and conflict can gradually destroy understanding and intimacy in a marriage. Without the feeling of being understood and appreciated, partners lose the pleasure and caring they once had in their marriage. When we can share our feelings and listen to each other, we can then spend our energy finding solutions to the real issues in the conflict.

Kathy married expecting a family of about five children. Since she and Jeff had not talked about children before marriage, she assumed Jeff also wanted a family. After the wedding, he told her that he did not intend to have children. Three painful years later, this issue split the couple, but also led to some counseling. When I asked Jeff if he really did not want children, he said he did not. Then I asked why he had not shared this with Kathy before marriage. He admitted fear that she would not marry him. When I asked Jeff why he did not want children, he replied, "I would never do to a child what my dad did to me!" This provided a key insight into his fear. Jeff quickly realized that he did like children but was afraid to repeat the pain of his own childhood. With counseling, they made the decision to have children. I remember Jeff's eagerness to introduce me to the children several years later.

Learning to deal with conflict is a process in which our initial goal is not to solve problems but to understand ourselves. When a relationship is healthy, we can generally solve issues or learn how to live with them. Some issues will continue, such as differences in personality or temperament. Sometimes we have not discovered the real issue, such as a fear of intimacy.

Learning to deal with conflict means being willing to experience pain so that we might become more aware and more loving. To do this, we need to believe in ourselves and in each other. We are both wounded people who need healing, and we can help each other to heal.

Conflict need not be the enemy of a marriage relationship. It can be an ally in gaining intimacy and understanding. Couples too often play it safe, avoiding conflict and the wounds that may occur. They don't confront the issues, and their relationship doesn't grow. If, after years of marriage, we have no scars from dealing with conflict, we need to ask ourselves, "Was there nothing worth fighting for?"

Reflection: How do I handle my feelings of anger? Do I get defensive or do I try to discover the deeper feelings behind my anger?

Sharing: How were conflicts handled in the home where I grew up? Am I repeating these patterns?

9

"Can I Ever Trust Again?"

Trust walks are common experiences on youth retreats. A young man was leading our confirmation class on a trust walk, taking them under tree limbs, up steep hills, and over obstacles. Finally, he took the thirty-five high schoolers onto the dock. Under their weight, the dock let go at the shore end and collapsed slowly into the lake. The youths screamed as they sank to their armpits in water, but they hung on because they believed it was part of the trust walk.

Children seem to trust quite naturally, both physically and emotionally, until their trust is shut down by external events. Parents or others may have told them, "Trust me," and then failed to prove trustworthy. This leaves them confused and wary. Mistrust builds up over time. When we are hurting, we tend to remember times when our trust was betrayed. This impedes our ability to trust.

A young couple already living together were preparing for their wedding. She was wishing they could separate for the two months remaining before their wedding. Their sponsor couple approved of this idea, and asked her why she didn't move out of the apartment. "I'd never trust him!" she replied. Behind this woman's response was likely a fear of inadequacy or rejection.

Fear is the enemy of trust. We don't want to get hurt, so we protect ourselves, putting up barriers to relationship, and miss out on the most intimate relationship spouses can have. The hurts that cause us pain and make us withdraw come from many sources. When a person feels manipulated or used by another, a barrier builds that stymies trust. Often our fear of being hurt again is stronger than the desire for a close relationship with the person who hurt us.

In troubled marriages, communication becomes sparse. We avoid touchy areas, talking about issues rather than about what each is suffering inside. Making ourselves known to someone else, especially sharing something we don't like about ourselves, causes us all kinds of fears. These fears make us want to run away. They paralyze us so that we cannot reveal our inner selves. We need to find ways to open ourselves to the other in trust again.

We need to identify and be in touch with our fears if we are to overcome them and develop confidence in ourselves. As long as my focus is inward, concentrating on myself and my fears, I will be in a battle against myself. I will be caught in a tug of war between my fears and the need to reveal myself honestly with others.

A powerful example of the struggle to trust appears in the gospels. Peter and the other disciples were caught in a storm at sea, certain they would drown, when Jesus walked by their boat. At first they thought he was a ghost and cried out in fear. When someone recognized Jesus, Peter shouted, "Lord, if it is really you, tell me to come to you across the water." "Come," Jesus invited. So Peter got out of the boat and began walking across the water toward Jesus. Growing conscious of the strong wind and the breaking waves, Peter got frightened, lost his trust, and down he went.

As long as Peter kept his eyes on Jesus, he could walk on the water but, when fear drew him into himself, he lost that ability. In a similar way, when our focus is on another, we can usually share deeply of our feelings. When we become self-conscious, we grow fearful like Peter and sink into self-protection.

Trust Is a Decision

Placing our trust in someone who has the power to hurt us is the scariest thing we are asked to do. Trust, like love, is not a feeling but a decision. We rise above our feelings of fear, jealousy, or panic and don't allow ourselves to be controlled by such feelings. We do not make a decision to let go of the fear. We make a decision to trust in spite of our fear and to concentrate on the present. Nobody else can make that decision for us.

Trust enables us to share feelings that we have difficulty telling others about. We take a chance on being open and honest. Trust allows us to act despite our hesitations, to believe in the goodness of another despite our fear, and to believe in what others tells us.

We freely make a choice to trust our spouse or others and to let them into our life. Trust begets trust. In other words, we can develop an attitude of trust if we start practicing being open. Only when I trust in someone will I find the joy of being understood, the peace of being accepted, and the feeling of closeness.

Psychologists point out that trust is made up of three components—honesty, acceptance, and respect. Trust also brings with it the responsibility of being trustworthy, behaving in a way that will earn our spouse's trust.

Couples in trouble grow defensive and wary, believing they will never be able to trust again. Dialogue enables couples to build a deeper trust in each other and to share many difficult feelings in their relationship. The decision to be vulnerable or transparent, and to share openly and honestly, is a powerful experience. People discover that they no longer need to be imprisoned in their feelings. Mental struggles, such as "What will he think of me after hearing this?" or "Will she use this against me in the future?" diminish when spouses feel each other's acceptance.

Mary was an incest victim, unable to share with her husband not only the experience but her feelings of shame and fear of discovery. Her abuser had warned that whoever learned what she had done would know how bad she was. Ten years into their marriage, Mary struggled to reveal her painful secrets to me in counseling. In time, I asked her to tell Kenneth, since her brokenness was being reflected in her sexual responses. Mary panicked, fearing Kenneth's rejection. Yet, she agreed to be honest, sensing her feelings presented a barrier to intimacy. Kenneth listened lovingly to her pain, to her fears and feelings about herself, accepting and supporting her with his love even when she confronted her abuser. Now that Mary feels secure knowing Kenneth still respects her, she is gradually sharing more deeply about her feelings of shame and entrusting herself to him sexually with new freedom.

An atmosphere of trust is essential to good, intimate communication. Trust and openness in any relationship have to be a conscious and deliberate choice. I remember the first time that I shared my own struggles with prayer in a homily. I had to make a decision to trust the congregation, but it wasn't easy.

People expect a priest to be a man of prayer, so I felt very inadequate and somewhat a failure as I shared that it isn't always easy for me to pray, that I often give work priority over prayer, and often pray routinely because my mind has been distracted by other concerns and anxieties. As I shared these struggles as honestly as I could, I felt very vulnerable. I wasn't sure the parishioners would understand.

As I stopped to shake people's hands at the rear of the church, I still felt uneasy until it was all over and I realized what had happened. Several of the elderly ladies stopped to thank me and give me a big hug on the way out. When I left church after unvesting, four couples were waiting outside to get into a discussion about prayer. People rarely stop to discuss the homily, so I realized the gift of trusting them with my struggles and fears rather than giving them another intellectual talk about prayer. I felt affirmed and accepted, knowing that I could share myself as I was.

Affirmation plays an important role in the growth of trust. We have countless opportunities to affirm each other. Spouses depend on each other to reflect their worth. If we call each other names or insult and criticize each other, we won't believe we have any self-worth. If we only praise each other for achievements, we may believe we are loved only for what we do, rather than for who we are.

True affirmation in a relationship means living our lives together with a sense of care and concern for each other. Our attitude conveys affirmation and love. It will also be shown through actions such as staying close at a party, listening well, acknowledging our love, or giving each other the gift of our precious time.

Real trust doesn't happen overnight. When trust has been betrayed, the recovery process, even with counseling, is painfully slow. Trust is always a risk, especially when we're trying to put the pieces of our relationship back together after trust is broken. Twelve Step programs advise living "one day at a time." This means not being overwhelmed by the problem that marred our trust, but deciding what we can do today to begin to trust again. Broken trust is mended with commitment, dialogue, time, and forgiveness.

Trust begins when we learn to listen within ourselves. Being able to be ourselves with each other, without pretense, will bring a sense of freedom and intimacy for both of us.

Reflection: How do I feel trusting my spouse with my deepest feelings?

Sharing: What topic do I find most difficult to talk about with my spouse? What fears within me make the topic a difficult one?

10

Will You Forgive Me?

Very early in our lives we learned some magic words. Perhaps it happened when we asked for a cookie. Mom handed it to us and then suddenly jerked it back, asking "What do you say first?" Once we said "Please," got the cookie, and turned to leave, mom stopped us again by asking: "When I give you something, what do you say?" "Please" and "Thank you" were necessary to survive childhood. We had to say the magic words of childhood, whether we really meant them or not, to get what we wanted.

There are some magic words in marriage too. These words are, "I'm sorry. Please forgive me" and "I forgive you." Sometimes we think we can use these words like the magic words of childhood. We don't mean them, but saying them gets us what we want. If we ask forgiveness to feel good again, or to make our spouse feel good, or to improve the atmosphere around the house, we are taking a step in the right direction by making life more livable. But this is not the essence of forgiveness.

Hurt and suffering are a very real part of every life. Many married couples carry their hurts around, adding to them regularly, storing them up so that they can be called to the surface at a moment's notice. Opportunities occur daily for forgiveness because family members live in such close proximity. Forgiveness is essential in resolving marital breakdown.

I think we struggle with forgiveness because we have not understood reconciliation well as Christians. For years Catholics placed the emphasis of the sacrament of reconciliation on confession of sin. A gracious God forgave whatever we asked. This put the emphasis on the sinner's actions rather than on God's healing. The sacrament is a moment of healing the sinner, who has failed and needs to be reconciled. It is also a channel of God's graces, which helps us turn from our sinfulness and change our lives.

Jesus' story of the Prodigal Son challenges our understanding of reconciliation. The father, although hurt by his son's selfish behavior, rushes out to forgive the errant son and welcome him back into the family. Forgiveness is the responsibility of the one who has been hurt. Jesus' story offers us many insights on the healing power of forgiveness for troubled marriages.

"Love Forgives All Things"

The hardest funeral I ever celebrated was that of a nineteen-year-old youth killed in a snowmobile accident. The family's bitterness toward the pickup driver who struck the young man put a real damper on the wake and funeral. I didn't know what to do with their unforgiveness and bitterness.

Two weeks later I listened to the noted author Christianne Brusselmans describe her nephew's funeral. Twenty-one-year-old John was picked up by his nineteen-year-old friend, Paul, who wanted to show off his father's new car. Paul went speeding on wet gravel country roads on a sloppy, rainy night with two other youths in the car. Seated in the back seat, John had for a third time just said: "For God's sake, Paul, slow down. You're going to kill us all!" when the car spun out of control. John died immediately.

When Paul returned to his parents' home that evening, they blurted out in frustration, "You can't stay here because you just murdered your best friend!"

Three days later, at the funeral planned by John's brothers, fifteen and seventeen years old, Paul appeared in the sanctuary in those early moments of the Mass where we ask God's forgiveness. Supported by the two brothers, Paul asked John's parents for forgiveness and the brothers answered, "Lord, have mercy." Then he asked John's eight brothers and sisters, his grandparents, and other relatives for forgiveness and the brothers responded "Christ, have mercy." Finally, Paul asked the adults present to forgive the foolish sins of all youth. Some of the congregation, now grasping what was happening, joined in the "Lord, have mercy."

John's mother, not expecting this moment but moved by Paul's words, pulled her husband out of the pew and into the sanctuary to forgive Paul. They embraced him, and realizing that Paul's parents had not forgiven him, took Paul between them to ask his parents to reconcile. Paul's parents were now able to forgive and embrace their son. The priest celebrating the funeral, who was also unaware this would happen, caught the spirit of the moment and invited everyone to reach out to a spouse, a child, a parent, or a neighbor with whom they needed reconciliation. The entire congregation responded by moving throughout the church to forgive and ask forgiveness.

Christianne's story was very helpful to me two months later. This time I was celebrating a funeral with my family. A twenty-three-year-old nurse was giving her five-year-old nephew a bicycle ride when a young man on his way to a wedding dance struck and killed them. The driver's presence, along with his parents, was very important at the funeral. It's such a terrible experience to kill someone accidentally, and the heavy burden of guilt lingers. We needed to heal him as much as possible. But we also needed him there so we could get rid of our anger and pain rather than carry resentment and bitterness in our lives.

This holds a lesson for forgiveness in marriage. Marriages often break down because of an accumulation of hurts from indifference, insensitivity, retaliation, physical abuse, criticism, nagging, or hurting the other to get attention. When we get hurt, the pain makes us turn in on ourselves, focusing on the pain rather than on the other person. The one who is hurt and the one who did the hurting both need healing. We have to tell the other person we forgive and be certain the other accepts forgiveness. Forgiveness is not the same as forgetting our hurt. We need to forgive precisely because our memory keeps the pain long after the actual wrongdoing. When we forgive, we can give up the feelings that have helped us hang onto the hurt.

When someone injures us and we hold onto the hurt, we can't love. Without forgiveness, we are busy with resentment. When we injure someone and we curl up in guilt, we turn inward, with too much pride to say "I'm sorry," or too paralyzed by dislike of self to move outward. We can choose to stay where we are, or we can give and ask forgiveness. Forgiveness is a decision, not a feeling. Forgiveness frees both parties to love and to grow. For-

giveness asks us to take a risk, to make ourselves vulnerable, and to renew our commitment to a spouse who
has betrayed our trust even though we fear being hurt
again.

We can forgive each other and accept forgiveness
only when we can forgive ourselves. We use many excuses
for the way we behave instead. Excusing is the opposite of
forgiveness, because it denies blame. We tell ourselves we
act this way because of others or because experiences in
our past cause us to behave the way we do. We need to
look underneath our excuses and take responsibility for
our actions. Only then can we forgive ourselves for having
acted badly. We need to get beyond our pride or fear of
rejection or humiliation, which keeps us from giving up
the terrible burden of unforgiveness.

In every broken relationship, both partners are
responsible for some degree of hurt. Both are hurting,
because one carries the wound and the other carries the
guilt. The one carrying the wound does not easily give up
the load, which does not allow the spouse to give up the
guilt.

Often a spouse does not even know the hurts we
carry. Big hurts are often dealt with, while the little hurts
from being taken for granted, moments of indifference,
critical words, and all the little infidelities of relationship
linger in our feelings. If a partner is aware of inflicting hurt
on the other, he or she should sincerely ask forgiveness.
Saying "I'm sorry" simply means "I made a mistake,
please excuse me." Asking "Will you forgive me?" recognizes a broken relationship. Often a person does not know
that he or she has caused a hurt, which puts the responsibility for beginning the healing process on the one who
has been hurt.

Sometimes hurts are so great that it is impossible to
find the resources within ourselves to forgive. At those
times we need to ask God to work through us to forgive

the one who has wounded us. When St. Paul reminds us that "Love forgives all things," he is talking about the gift of the Holy Spirit that helps us to be forgiving.

The Process of Healing

Healing from serious hurts is a process involving more than forgiveness. We have all been hurt, whether by our parents, our spouse, our children, or the many other people whose lives interact with ours. What we do with these hurts makes a difference in our lives. When we are hurt, we tend to reject others, closing off communication and intimacy, or to develop an indifference toward others. The process of achieving forgiveness and healing very often goes through several stages.

The first stage, *denial*, happens because the pain is so severe we don't want to deal with it. People give themselves messages such as "It wasn't that bad," or "Other people have it worse," stuffing the pain by pretending that everything is fine. Good Christians may speak of carrying their cross. Denial keeps us from looking at what has happened to us or what we have done to another, often because we feel like damaged goods.

We move out of denial by admitting what happened and taking ownership of it. People experiencing difficulty identifying where they are hurt may need to go through a review of their life. Close attention should be given to acts of omission in their relationships, such as a lack of closeness and intimacy. We can look also at our own attitudes, such as "It doesn't affect me." We go back to remember not only the incidents that happened, but to recall how we defended ourself by setting aside our pained reaction. We missed expressing our feelings at the crucial time because it was too painful or because the person who hurt us would not allow us to be angry or sad.

Self-blame frequently overwhelms us when we admit what happened. We tell ourselves "It was my fault," or "If only I had done differently, this wouldn't have happened to me." Our parent, we rationalize, abandoned us because we were bad, or our spouse abuses us because of our personality.

We need to sort out what really was our responsibility in this situation. If the hurt happened to us as a child, most responsibility rests on the parent or adult who hurt us. If others have told us that the hurt was our fault, we may now believe that everything that goes wrong in our lives happens because something is wrong with us. In this stage, we often tell ourselves, "I deserve it because . . ." We need to externalize our shame by owning it and then uncovering its sources so we can give it back to the person who shamed us.

A *victim* mentality often replaces self-blame. We begin to put the blame where it belongs, naming the person who hurt us, but we feel powerless so we stress our role as victims with "poor me" statements. We may act out by hurting someone other than the one who hurt us, or by self-indulgence with food and alcohol. We may demand special treatment from others.

We move beyond the victim stage by self-discipline, replacing the chaos in our lives with order and care for ourselves. We need to move beyond a sense of generalized pain to focus clearly on just what the hurt was. We might write a description of our hurt, describing in a paragraph the actual incident of who did what to us and another paragraph on how we felt then. We can write another paragraph on how we feel right now, trying to get below surface feelings to our strongest feelings. We often want those who have hurt us to change so that we won't be the victims of their behavior again. We will heal faster, however, by working instead on our own healing. They may not change, but as healed people we will be able to love them the way they are.

Anger, focused on the person who hurt us, often follows the victim stage. Anger energizes powerless victims to start protecting themselves and to set clearer boundaries in the relationship so others can't hurt them again. People at this stage need to be responsible in how they express their anger. Rage is anger out of control. To recognize our anger, we can ask whether we take our anger out on family members. Do we withhold love and affection? Do we seek to punish others by our behavior? Are we physically abusive? Have others pointed to our angry behavior to suggest that we change or go to counseling? Once we recognize and take ownership of our anger, we need to look deeper into the feelings behind the anger if we are to let go of it.

A *survivor* mentality moves us beyond anger. A survivor can look at what happened and celebrate the growth that results from moving through the pain. Survivors recognize that they did what they could at the time and that the person who hurt them was also doing his or her best with limited resources. Survivors often want to help others, especially through such groups as adult children of alcoholics, victims of adultery, or victims of domestic abuse. Our stories need to be told in order to move us on. Sharing our story enhances a spiritual awakening as we come to a deeper insight into our being.

Wholeness and healing come as we understand what happened and how it affected us. We are more than the hurts others did to us, more than our brokenness. Forgiveness enables us to let go, find peace, and move on. Forgiveness means putting aside our hurts to focus on our beloved. Such deep inner forgiveness is a grace from God, achieved through prayer and the decision to love.

Reconciliation brings new life and inner peace. We have the power to heal each other through forgiveness.

When someone I have hurt reaches out to me, especially before I have mustered the courage to ask forgiveness, it is a very life-giving moment.

Reflection: When have I experienced healing in being forgiven?

Sharing: How have my decisions to forgive my spouse affected our relationship?

11

"How Often Should a Couple Make Love?"

Mark Twain once quipped: "Niagara Falls is the second biggest disappointment to honeymooners." Too often, the sexual relationship remains a disappointment through much of marriage. Couples with struggling relationships may avoid sex or only use each other for sexual pleasure.

Our sexuality is one of God's most powerful and beautiful gifts. Sexuality is God's way of calling us out of our aloneness into relationship. Sexuality is not limited to intercourse. It is an integral part of who we are as men and women which shows in much of what we do in life. Sexuality involves my view of myself. If we are psychologically or emotionally alienated from our sexuality we will be handicapped in pursuit of human intimacy. A healthy level of comfort with our sexuality contributes much to our ability to relate successfully with others. Ultimately, our sexuality relates closely to our spirituality.

Sexuality for each of us involves more than physical excitement. We tend to compartmentalize sex in our lives, as if it was an area apart from the whole relationship. Then we run the risk of using sex to manipulate each other. We give sex as a reward, withhold it as a punishment, and try new techniques to make it exciting when it gets boring.

Men fear failure, especially with respect to sexuality. If a man admits that he doesn't know everything about sex, he feels he has failed. So he wears a "know-it-all" mask, but underneath he may have self-doubts. When his wife asks for a backrub but doesn't want to have intercourse, he feels confused. He associates sex with intercourse and doesn't see this as an expression of his sexuality.

A woman ties lovemaking to her self-image. If she was sexually abused as a child, feels guilt about past sexual experiences, or doesn't find her husband romantic, she will be less enthusiastic. When a man focuses on his needs and fails to affirm his wife's attractiveness, she often feels used. She may think that he just wants her body, failing to see how much sex is tied to his need to express himself.

Sex provides a unique way to communicate ourselves to each other. Unfortunately, we see sex as something we do rather than an expression of who we are and what we mean to each other. Psychologists give us the Marital Intimacy Scale, which says that the quality of a couple's sexual relationship depends largely upon the quality of their total relationship, which depends largely upon the quality of their communication, which in turn depends largely upon the quality of their openness and listening. A couple wishing to improve their sexual life, then, also needs to work on their openness and listening.

We tend to think of the quantity or number of times we have sex rather than the quality of our sexual lovemaking. Love, wanting the very best for our partner, is focused on the other person. For example, a loving, considerate husband temporarily forgets about his needs to concentrate on the pleasure he can give his wife.

Several years ago, a *Redbook* report on women and sexuality surprised many Americans. *Redbook* found that the more religious a woman is, the more she enjoys sex, initiates lovemaking, and the more frequently the couple make love. A headline announcing the article read: "Religious Women More Sexually Satisfied." I tell the men on Engaged Encounter weekends that the moral of this article is to make certain they marry a religious woman.

I remember Michelle, a young wife of two years, expressing her hurt and frustration. Michelle said: "It really bothers me, the way people make fun of sex. I've never heard anyone make fun of a beautiful sunset. And, to me, making love with Art is more beautiful than any sunset." Michelle is right. God made our bodies male and female, sexual and exciting, as a gift to us.

Too often we fail to connect sex with love and with God. Actually, the model for a couple's sexuality is the eucharist. As Jesus offers himself, "This is my body . . . given in love for you," so husband and wife are saying by their gift that ". . . this is my body given in love." Then the sexual act becomes a ritual of their unity and a sacramental moment.

Sexual activity detached from commitment and care for the partner usually leads to alienation rather than intimacy. Marriage offers the ideal relationship in which sexual activity can become sexual intimacy enjoyed with love, trust, and continuity. The sexual side of marriage suffers when conflicts are unresolved, while a healthy relationship finds full expression in sexual activity. What happens in the kitchen is brought into the bedroom. Sexual intimacy becomes a reflection of a couple's total intimacy.

Intimacy

We often think of intimacy as physical closeness, involving sexual activities. But intimacy is much more than that. While sex is one way of being intimate with another, partners who attempt to create intimacy by sexual activity often end up frustrated. Pain, suffering, and loneliness are often forerunners of intimacy. Intimate partners feel understood, accepted, appreciated, cared for, and loved.

Most people hope to find intimacy in marriage. However, intimacy doesn't just happen. Genuine intimacy occurs when both partners have a desire for a deep relationship, and both are willing to make the effort to achieve closeness. Deep closeness is bought at the high cost of sharing our life with another. Deep intimacy can be achieved only when a couple are willing to fight about what is important, including their sexual relationship.

In marriage a man and woman not only live under the same roof but open their lives completely to each other. Many fear the pain, the honesty, and the humility that characterize deep human relationships; yet never before has marriage been expected to produce such a high quality of interpersonal relationships. More breakdowns, separations, and divorces than ever result because the demand for intimacy in marriage is so overwhelming.

Intimacy means we become vulnerable and transparent enough to allow another to touch us at the deepest levels of our being. We must be prepared to let a relationship change us. We enter into a long and continuous process of self-revelation. We must become known and know each other in a unique way, even though we may not be readily disposed to open ourselves to the profound risks of intimacy or prepared to work through the painful process of change called for in the intimate encounter of married life.

All of us have a need to feel close to another person. But anxiety about letting anyone get too close to us often becomes a barrier to intimacy. As we begin to feel the warmth of closeness, we may also feel vulnerable because we are afraid our partner will dislike or reject us. Since many of us fear being exposed as weak, inadequate, or inferior, we become defensive to avoid too much intimacy. We may also feel apprehensive about being swallowed up in the relationship, especially if our sense of self is poorly developed or insecure.

Fear of abandonment may also hamper intimacy. An adult whose childhood has been marked by excessive or traumatic separations, such as divorce or the death of a parent, makes an unconscious link between intimacy and loss. Intimacy stirs unconscious fears of being traumatically separated. They often defend themselves against the threat of intimacy by generating conflict.

Intimacy requires trust. Trust assures that my best interests will be taken into account. When we trust, we can tell our partner our deepest feelings, fears, and hopes, and know that they will be handled with care. Trust between marriage partners can develop only in an atmosphere of mutual commitment. Trust grows as both partners communicate by their words and actions that their relationship gets high priority. Trust provides the safe climate needed for intimacy.

Our desire to be in union with a spouse is also a desire to be in union with God's life in us. God created us male and female as two parts of a whole. Although two become one, intimacy holds an element of separateness. A healthy degree of separateness strengthens intimacy; our individual gifts, interests, and activities enrich our life together. Sharing intimacy with a spouse presumes that we are in touch with our own soul and that we respect that part of our spouse. We are persons of equal dignity, each a son or daughter of God. Intimacy is not clinging dependence nor controlling domination, but a linking of two separate individuals.

Doing what we want and need for ourselves while caring deeply for our partner isn't always easy. We must cherish our freedom while respecting our spouse's freedom. When we care deeply enough for a spouse to explore how he or she is affected by our behavior, and stand ready to help a spouse understand the fears that arise in the face of our freedom, intimacy deepens. A truly intimate relationship demands that both partners feel the freedom to live their lives in ways that satisfy each of them while still meeting the other's needs.

Intimate love encourages us to share our natural, spontaneous feelings. A spouse willing to share his or her deepest feelings with us and be affected by us helps us feel important. Knowing our partner is essential to intimacy, but by itself is not enough for us to feel loved. We also need our partner to know us, to see and understand who we are. The more of our personality we expose and feel accepted for, the more deeply loved we will feel. As we feel loved, we become more willing to lower our protections and expose more of our hidden selves. Openly sharing our painful feelings and receiving the warmth and acceptance of our spouse is profoundly intimate.

Most couples discover that they frequently build walls between themselves. Anger often causes resentments, which create a distance and make us defensive with each other. Expectations and unwillingness to change, poor communication skills, and low self-esteem are other barriers to intimacy. Lack of self-awareness often limits our understanding of and sensitivity toward another. The pressures in our lives create tensions and fatigue, which block our response to others.

We need to take steps toward building intimacy. Recognizing and building on intimacy present in a relationship is a good place to start. Time is an important element of intimacy. Our frantic pace and accompanying fatigue often make it impossible to share our feelings. Spending time with one another provides one of the best ways of showing that we value our spouse and our marriage. Recommitment to the growth of a relationship, becoming partners in building self-esteem and trust, learning to share feelings, getting rid of anger and resentment, helping each other to take risks, and setting aside time for each other can help us become more intimate. A deep level of intimacy can be achieved in most marriages.

Sexual intimacy is delightful, affirming, and powerful when experienced in a context of a deeply loving relationship. In this time of busyness, alienated families, and high divorce, the church would be far richer if couples took more time for sexual intimacy.

In a sharing session with engaged couples, I was asked how often a couple should make love in marriage. I said, "Just follow the church's teaching." After a pause, one of them said: "You mean the church has a teaching on that too?" "Of course," I answered, "Catholic couples make love on days beginning with 'T'—Tuesday, Thursday, Triday, Taturday, Today, Tomorrow." Another young man quickly concluded: "Father, didn't you forget Tis-morning and Tis-afternoon?" I gave him a gold star.

Reflection: What do we need to do to increase our mutual openness and intimacy?

Sharing: How do I see our sexual intimacy helping to create unity in our marriage?

PART IV

SPIRITUALITY

12

"Isn't It Possible God Could Have Made a Mistake?"

During a Retrouvaille weekend, Julie asked to visit with me at lunch time on Sunday. She started by saying she wanted to show me what she wrote earlier in the weekend. In the "Encounter With Self" talk, I mentioned a civil rights era poster that pictured a three-year-old black lad in tattered clothing standing beside a falling down shack. A statement at the top of the picture said: "God made me." Beneath the child were the words: "And God doesn't make junk." I had suggested that each one of us needed to put these words on the mirror where we see ourself or on our picture to be reminded of who we are in God's sight.

Julie handed me her notebook opened to the page for "Encounter With Self." At the top of the page, she had

117

written: "Isn't it possible God could have made a mistake?" Below she had drawn a zero the size of her notebook, indicating that she was an absolute nothing. After showing me this page, Julie cried her eyes out as she said: "I don't feel that way any more." I was certain that she didn't as we continued to talk.

A similar story is told about a group of writers in a restaurant. They were discussing shame, and someone asked a question about the difference between guilt and shame. As they stumbled toward the answer, a young woman who had been sitting alone at a nearby table rose and started toward the cashier. As she passed their table, she said: "Guilt is when you make a mistake. Shame is when you are a mistake."

God doesn't make mistakes. Reflecting on the mystery of life, the author of Genesis noted how after completing the work of creation, "God looked at everything he had made, and he found it very good" (Gn 1:31). This image of the basic goodness of creation applies both to each of us individually and also to marriage. Genesis also says: "In the divine image he created him; male and female he created them" (1:27).

Jesus quotes this scripture passage to the Jews who are trying to trip him up in the last week of his life. When asked, "May a man divorce his wife for any reason whatever?" Jesus answered, "Have you not read that at the beginning the Creator made them male and female and declared, 'For this reason a man shall leave his father and mother and cling to his wife, and the two shall become as one'? Thus they are no longer two but one flesh. Therefore, let no man separate what God has joined" (Mt 19:3-6).

Unfortunately, we stop there and don't read the conclusion of the story where the Jews challenged Jesus' teaching. At that time there was a disagreement among the rabbis. Some said that a man could give his wife a writ of divorce for any reason, while others held that a man could divorce only for a major reason such as adultery. Women were property, without any rights, and could not divorce their husbands. Jesus reminded them that, because of the hardness of their hearts, Moses and their forefathers had allowed them to divorce and remarry, but it was not always that way. This scene ends with the Jews murmuring and leaving, while a rich young man comes to ask what he must do to be a disciple. Jesus liked the young man and asked him to give up his riches, which had distracted him from God. The young man left sadly because he could not make this commitment.

Scripture scholars tell us that what happened next refers to both events of the morning. The disciples are overwhelmed and ask Jesus: "Then who can be saved?" Jesus responds, "For man it is impossible; but for God all things are possible" (Mt 19:26). Jesus' focus in his teaching on marriage centers on what God has united, acknowledging that with God's gracious help all things are possible.

Statistics prove the wisdom of Jesus' teaching even today. While nearly two-thirds of all marriages end in divorce, I frequently hear speakers cite a U.S. Census Bureau statistic indicating that couples who belong to the same denomination, attend religious services at least weekly, and pray or read scripture together daily have a divorce rate of 1 in 1105. With God, all things are still possible.

God's Plan for Marriage

God does have a plan for married couples, namely that they find fulfillment in marriage. We talk about marriage as a vocation, which means that God has called these two persons into this relationship. I find that many couples have a deep sense of God's role in bringing them together. A couple's sense of worth comes from the One who called them to belong to each other. In the sacrament of marriage, couples are called to be a sacred sign of God's presence and action in their lives. Through their love relationship, they witness to the Christian community the truth of the claim: "This is how all will know you for my disciples: your love for one another" (Jn 13:35).

Even though the scriptures relate the holiness of God's plan for us, the church gradually began to adopt a popular philosophy that divided into the holy and the unholy, the sacred and the secular, the spiritual and the material. The spiritual was holy, as when people went off to the desert as hermits or to the monastery to pray. Material objects were unholy. The division of body and soul regarded the body and sex as material and therefore evil, and praised abstinence as holier than married sexuality. Eventually, celibacy was seen as a strength and marriage as a weakness. Marriage then became a second rate vocation rather than a way of living in God's own image. Thus, Christians escaped their homes and daily lives to find God in church. Clergy focused on the personal salvation of Christians rather than on their daily living in the world.

Although the preceding is certainly a caricature, it serves as a contrast to the biblical view of marriage and family life being recovered today. Now we recognize that the primary unit of the church is the family. Although we tend to think of marriage as something very ordinary, it is not ordinary when God calls a couple to be a powerful sign to each other and to the world as they become a community of love. I believe that the promise of Jesus, "Where two or three are gathered in my name, there am I in their midst" (Mt 18:20), refers in a special way to the family, which is sometimes called the domestic church.

Faith

On Saturday night of a Retrouvaille weekend, I told couples I would be available in the lounge next to my room. Soon a man came to ask: "Father, can you prove God to me? I'm an engineer, into science, and I need things proved."

"No," I answered, "I can't prove God to you. But, if you want God in your life, it won't happen because you find God. God will find you." I shared with him that for me faith is an experience *of* God rather than knowledge *about* God. Faith happens in key moments of life, when we are most in need and somehow conscious of God's presence in our lives. An old World War II axiom reminded us: "There are no atheists in foxholes." God finds us when we fall in love, when we wrestle with whether we are lovable enough that someone could commit to us for life. When we experience this kind of unconditional love, then we experience God who is love.

Childbirth provides another faith experience, as we hold that tiny infant and exclaim: "My God, this a miracle. It's more than the two of us!" Even death can be an encounter with God. When a parent dies, we may question the meaning of life. Even doubting can be a faith experience.

As a young seminarian, I remember seeing a graph that showed the physical and the emotional growth of a human. Physically we grow very fast after birth, reaching full physical maturity at about age twenty-four. But the spiritual growth graph did not look much different at age twenty-four than at age six. After thirty, the graph began to rise rapidly, while after fifty it skyrocketed.

After talking for half an hour, this seeker left believing that God would find him if he stayed open. Soon a couple came to talk. He began the conversation: "Father, can you help me? I'm an atheist and I have never believed in God. My partner's faith is her strength, and I want that faith." I asked him to tell me what he could about her faith. We also talked about faith as the experience of God's presence and action in our lives. He, too, left hoping God would catch up with him.

Sometimes our difficulty lies not with the presence of God but with the kind of God we face. Dying of cancer, Sharon had lived several weeks longer than the hospital staff thought possible. When I came to the hospital ward one day, a nurse told me Sharon seemed very afraid and asked if I would talk with her. I knew Sharon quite well, so I quickly asked her, "Sharon, are you afraid?"

"Yes!" she said quietly.

"Are you afraid of death?"

"No," she responded.

"Are you afraid of God?" When Sharon, a beautiful wife, mother, and active Catholic, affirmed that she was afraid of God, I thought perhaps it was because of her father. After talking a bit about her fear, I asked her to tell me about her father. She described him as an alcoholic, often harsh and unaffirming during her childhood years.

After talking about her father for a while, I asked Sharon to tell me about her husband as a father. She described Jerry as a devoted husband and good father, gentle with his children as well as with her. She was obviously excited and peaceful as she talked on about Jerry.

Finally, I said quietly: "Sharon, I am going to leave now, and I want you to spend some time thinking about God as Father in the image of Jerry." Sharon died that night.

Many people have to change their image of God, some because they identify God with a harsh, indifferent, or absent father, others because of hurts with the church. Alienated Catholics and, I presume, alienated persons of every faith, can tell others exactly when they were hurt by another member of the church. We expect the church to be perfect, but it isn't, even though it represents a loving God.

Forgiveness of these hurts is crucial to reconciliation with one's church and with God, just as reconciliation between spouses is essential for rebuilding marriages.

Prayer too is essential in our relationship with God. Yet many people have difficulty praying. In prayer we talk with God much like we talk to each other. Prayer is a dialogue with God about how I feel and what I need. Too often we simply throw a wish list at God when we feel need. Our relationship with God is then like a marriage in which only information is shared. In every conversation, including those with God, we need to listen. How does God speak to us? God speaks though a spouse or child, through the words of scripture, or directly to our mind, our heart, our will, or our feelings.

When a couple prays together, they let God into their relationship. Perhaps they pray for healing in their relationship. They may pray to be able to forgive and trust again. We can pray to learn how to listen well and not react, to be able to confront the dividedness in our hearts, or to know what God envisions for us. Such prayer can work wonders in the way we approach each other.

In 1 Corinthians 13, Paul tells us that we are not able to love unless the Spirit of God is active within us. Explaining that love is the highest gift of the Spirit, Paul reminds us that we cannot rise above our selfishness, our grudges, our lack of forgiveness, or other barriers to love unless we have God's help. A world of broken relationships needs to hear this in order to believe that God did not make a mistake in creating us or calling couples to live the holiness of a sacramental lifestyle.

Reflection: Do I feel hope for our relationship as I reflect on God's plan for marriage?

Sharing: What is my image of God? How do I feel about this?

13

Perfect Love Can Make Sacrifice a Joy

On a recent Phil Donahue show, panelists were trying to hang onto their marriages, claiming that their vows were for a lifetime, while the absent spouses wanted a divorce. The audience was ridiculing the guests, asserting that people had a right to be free from the marital commitment. Apparently, commitment has little meaning in our society.

In a writers' support group, I read an article I had written about the responsibility the church has to marriages in trouble. Charette liked the article, but commented that I held a counter-cultural stance. If believing in the promise to take each other for better or for worse, in good times and in bad, is counter-cultural, which certainly seems to be true, then the struggle to live a Christian marriage deserves special attention.

In our society's pattern for marriage, we marry for self-fulfillment. We expect someone to make us happy. We deserve to feel good. If our spouse doesn't make us happy, we will look elsewhere. Loneliness need not be tolerated. If things get rough, divorce is a way out. If the feeling of love goes dead, it's time to move on.

Jack met a married woman while on military reserve training. He came home to announce that he was leaving Sue and the four children. When I asked about his intentions, Jack answered that he wanted to do something just for himself. Jack's decision clearly reflected a "What's in it for me?" attitude rather than any concern about what this would do to the children, his parents, friends, and all those besides Sue who would be hurt by his decision.

Scripture presents Jesus' love for the church as the Christian model for marriage. In the fifth chapter of his letter to the Ephesians, St. Paul says that the love of a husband and wife is to be modeled on the love Jesus showed when he laid down his life for us. The Christian model for marriage reminds us that suffering and death will occur in every relationship. While so much of today's thinking centers on what we get out of marriage, St. Paul would remind us of the cost of building a relationship. Love asks "What can I do for you?" rather than "What's in it for me?"

Jesus experienced the four stages of a marriage relationship—romance, disillusionment, misery, and awakening to joy—in his relationship with his people. As he came to know who he was, Jesus had a deep sense of a Father who loved him and loved all people, and he willingly embraced his public ministry to these people. It didn't take long for him to experience disillusionment as his disciples tried to talk him out of his mission, while the Jewish religious and civic leaders plotted to get rid of him. Remember Jesus' plea: "O Jerusalem, Jerusalem, you slay the prophets and stone those who are sent to you! How often have I wanted to gather your children together as a mother bird collects her young under her wings, and you refused me!" (Lk 13:34). Who could miss the misery as Jesus prayed in the garden, "Father, if it is possible, let this cup pass me by!" or as he cried out in absolute aloneness on the cross, "My God, my God, why have you forsaken me?" Yet, Jesus continued to make the decision to love, which ultimately led to his resurrection and new life.

When we go through the disillusionment and misery stages, the other seems not to care, to be far off, or even to be the cause of our pain. We turn in on ourself rather than reaching out to our spouse in love. Disillusionment and misery happen in every relationship. The danger is that we can get stuck in the misery stage, not seeing the possibility of a better relationship and working to attain it. I have to die to myself, turning my focus from me to us, before I can experience the joy of the awakening stage.

Dying to self so that I can make the decision to love is never easy. I am prone to hang on to my hurts, my fears, my ways of protecting myself. I find it scary to reach out to the other person again, to decide to love. I feel even more hesitant to trust the other's love for me, to believe that I am lovable. I have to risk dying to all my self-protection.

The relationship cycle has two death stages and two resurrection stages. The romance or falling in love stage is characterized by new discoveries, closeness, attraction, intensity, personal and mutual affirmation. In the settling down or disillusionment stage, we begin to live everyday struggles and we start falling into routine. We may take our love for granted, and often we get more involved in work and other outside activities. The bottoming out or misery stage means crisis, distance, poor communication, anger, and hurt. In these death stages, I must in turn die to self before I can enter into a healthy relationship. In the beginning again or awakening to joy stage, forgiveness, acceptance, rebuilding, and attempting to change bring life back into the relationship.

For Better or for Worse

A recent ad for jewelry in the *Minneapolis Star* read: "*What to do with the jewelry your first husband gave you.*" It went on: "Whether it's the bracelet what's-his-name gave you that reminds you of a handcuff, or the ring that should've gone in his nose . . . we want it even if you don't." In the marriage model of society, suffering and death are to be avoided at all costs. If you don't make me happy, or if marital bliss disappears, I want out.

Despite this message, Christians vow to love no matter how difficult. We promise to make the decision to love not only in good times but also in the midst of a serious illness, a job loss, a drinking problem, or a conflict of interests. When we can reach out to each other in difficult times, we create a moment of awakening to joy. This is the model for marriage given us by Jesus, where love means looking toward the good of the other and laying down one's life for the other. Although this sounds hard, the result is new life, our own resurrection.

Marriage is not a steel trap, although we do a lot of struggling, and often feel disappointment that it is not all we thought it to be. Love, which seemed so strong before marriage, seems to elude our grasp as we blend into the ordinariness of humdrum life. Spouses often comment that marriage "has its ups and downs." The ups happen when love is visible and conscious. In the down times, love seems lost. After the powerful freedom we felt as we were falling in love, marriage turns out to be a daily challenge to make an almost impossible decision to love. Marriage involves a continual daily renewal of a decision so staggering that it can only be made through the grace of God.

"Falling in love," whether we realize it or not, is a

revelation from God. We receive a new vision of the power and potential of life, and have to decide how much we will let our lives be governed by this vision. Moving from love to marriage is a deep step in faith. We stake our life on a spiritual experience. Obviously, this is not something we can do for ourselves. This is a God-given vision that comes to us through our beloved. The experience is so earth shattering that we dedicate the rest of our lives to pursuing and enjoying the vision, vowing "till death do us part." If we stop loving before death, we regress into a belief that love is no enduring reality but a passing fancy or an illusion. We will have rejected and invalidated one of the deepest spiritual experiences of our lives.

Love has such power to change our entire life. Some people go into marriage thinking that they will not have to change much. When the terrifying process of change sets in, they dig in their heels and refuse to budge, and the ensuing tug of war creates disaster for their comfortable existence.

Marriage, even under the best circumstances, is a major life crisis. Whether this turns out to be a healthy, challenging opportunity or a disastrous nightmare depends largely upon how willing we are to be changed. Love has a transforming power for even the most comfortable and crusty. We are not simply moving in with someone new and exciting. We are giving assent to a whole chain reaction of trials, decisions, and transformations that may well change us beyond recognition.

By building up and celebrating life, love specializes in the destruction of something powerful and unyielding, namely our ego. Love calls us out of the secure darkness of our selfishness, and becomes the purest manifestation of selfhood. In fact, love is the only state in which the true self can exist. When the illegitimate self founded on pride and self-protection comes up against intimate love, it cannot stand. Our barriers crumble with shame, relief, and new insight. Love demonstrates convincingly that the real goal of self can only be achieved by way of total self-sacrifice.

Love creates the only safe ground upon which our self-assertion and self-protection may begin to be surrendered. As long as we are consumed in the struggle to be loved, we cannot love. The power to love derives solely from the knowledge that we are already loved. The best marriages grow out of the startling discovery that we can do nothing to earn love, and even more startling, that we can do nothing to keep ourselves from being loved.

Telling each other we are loved is not always an easy task. Sometimes when a spouse says, "I love you," it is not what the other wants to hear. We may be tired of hearing it. We may not want to think about what it means. We may not want to let go of whatever keeps us from accepting it.

In spite of all the resistance, the words of love are important. We need to speak of love when we are aware of the other's beauty and goodness, but even more when telling another they are loved seems almost impossible. We need to speak love in times of strife and hurt, or when the other's weakness is painfully apparent. At such times, an "I love you" can be a profound surprise even to the one who says these words. Such painful moments, every bit as much as moments of joy and beauty, occasion real love.

Unity

The goal of marriage is unity. This was also Jesus' goal for his followers. At the Last Supper, Jesus prayed "that all may be one as you, Father, are in me, and I in you." The unity stage in marriage is the awakening to joy stage. Thus, unity comes after the disillusionment and misery stages, as spouses die to their self-interests and self-protection to make the decision to love. We cannot avoid disillusionment and misery, but we can learn to recognize what is happening at these times. In this way we won't get stuck there, but we'll make the decision to reach out to each other in love.

Unity means we work through problems to achieve a oneness again. We become "we" centered rather than "I" centered. To be truly happy in marriage, we need to experience unity. Such unity is difficult to achieve. I often want to pull back from the other. I may lie a bit to save face. I may blame the other rather than admit my anger or insecurity. These are barriers to unity. When I make the decision to love instead, I may find it painful but in the end I will find joy. Love demands honesty and trust. Love requires sacrifice. We all fear sacrifice. But unity, which implies accepting the other person and giving the gift of myself, is the stern condition for succeeding at love. Perfect love can make sacrifice a joy.

St. Paul reminds us that such love is a gift of the Holy Spirit, not something coming from our own strength or goodness. The model for our love is Christ's love—not the sentimental love of popular songs but something strong and beautiful. Some of the deeper moments of unity are experienced around painful moments such as the death of a parent or child, an illness, a job loss, or a time of painful decisions.

When we work through a difficulty together, we come closer to each other and to God because we have learned to love more. St. Paul reminds us, "There is no limit to love's forbearance, to its trust, its hope, its power to endure. Love never fails."

Reflection: What is my concept of unity? What might we do to increase unity in our marriage?

Sharing: How do I feel about committing myself to love my spouse totally, knowing there will be times when I will get nothing in return?

14

"This Is My Body, Given for You"

By the symbolic use of bread at the Last Supper, Jesus realized a close link between Christian eucharist and Christian marriage. When he said, "This is my body, given for you," he combined the two most central symbols of human love and concern into one action. Jesus took the giving of food, the most basic action of parents as a mother nurses her baby or a family gathers around the table, and united its symbolism with that of the gift of our bodies in marital intercourse.

Sacraments are meant to be a special way we see into the reality and presence of God. The sacramentality of human love and self-giving touches the most basic level of this revelation. Sacramentality seems to be a universal experience among faith-filled married couples. American Catholics questioned about where they most find God in their lives responded ". . . in my marriage and family."

Although they may not be able to describe what it means to be a sacrament, most couples have moments when they realize they are in the presence of a mystery greater than themselves. These may be such moments as discovering a first pregnancy, childbirth, an intimate sexual experience, or reconciliation after a painful misunderstanding.

Speaking of God's creation, the book of Genesis says that humans were made in the image and likeness of God. The author then adds, "male and female God created them," telling us that the imaging of God occurs precisely in the relationship between humans, above all in the interaction of men and women. Knowledge of God can be gained in experiencing the relationship of husband and wife.

The Genesis text adds a further understanding that from this relationship life is to spread over the earth. In their relationship to one another, humans are to nurture life. If life is to extend to further life, either by creating new life or by creating new levels of personal life in people, it will happen on the basis of people's self-giving to one another.

Marriage as Sacrament

Marriage is a vocation, a call from God that acknowledges that the Creator has a plan for couples in marriage. The goal of this call is unity, becoming one in mind, heart, and affections. Perhaps the most difficult truth to believe over the course of our lifetime is that we are important enough to be loved by God. Nothing makes this more credible than our discovery of being important to and loved by another person. If we experience the love and care that others have for us, beginning with an infant's experience of parental love, and experience our own concern for others, we have some sense of how God might relate to us.

In the Old Testament, Hosea used the example of a husband's love for his wife as the image of Yahweh's love for the people of Israel. Jesus used another family comparison: "If you, with all your sins, know how to give your children what is good, how much more will your heavenly Father . . . "(Mt 7:11).

Our experience of human love in relationship, of being truly personal with and for one another, is sacramental. The human friendships we enjoy embody God's love for us. God works through all experiences of human love. Our consciousness of being loved both humanly and divinely leads us to the full personhood that is our destiny. Wholeness leads to holiness.

St. Paul adds another dimension of meaning to the relationship of husband and wife. In the letter to the Ephesians (5:21-32), Paul suggests that the relationship between the risen Christ and the Christian community must be the model for a loving relationship between the Christian couple. The self-giving of Jesus is understood in the bodily self-giving of husband and wife. Similarly, we are to understand the gift of self in marriage in terms of Jesus' death and resurrection. As Jesus moved into a new life of resurrection by full openness to the Spirit, so a Christian married couple is meant to move into a new and somewhat unexpected oneness, which cannot come to be unless each is willing to die to the more individualistic and less related way of life they had before.

In their relationship to one another, the couple are a sacrament to each other and a sacrament to those who know them. In this relationship, a Christian man and woman are truly "grace" to one another.

The Christian family is meant to be the most basic instance of Christian community—people bonded together by their shared relationship to the risen Jesus.

Family life is also very challenging, because intimacy and community are hard to achieve. But faith is a living relationship with our God. Many deep faith moments happen within marriage and family. Even the misery stage of a marriage can become a faith moment as we realize we are powerless and have an overwhelming need for God.

Family is an experience in community. The reality of "us" transcends the individuals in the family, whether we talk of the dynamic interactions or the spirit that animates the family's life. Families promote the growth in individuality of each member while calling for the participation and loving energy of all. In this cooperation something mysterious and powerful is created which transcends and enlivens the members of that community. Members live with and for each other as they recognize that their individuality contributes to and is enhanced by the rest of the community. The whole reveals God's creative capacity, without denying the unique and irreplaceable quality of each. As the family breaks bread together, members open themselves to each other and begin to live as one body. As we learn to share our lives at deep levels, we become aware that we are the body of Christ.

As the body of Christ, we are called to follow Jesus' example of ministry. He loved his followers with an act of service, washing their feet at the Last Supper, and he asked them—and us—to do the same. Our call to minister is a call to serve one another in love. Where do we find better footwashing ministry than in washing babies' bottoms, doing the family laundry, struggling with budget shortages, listening patiently to teenagers who color their hair orange, or taking in aging grandparents?

Ministry is a response to others' needs. Evy took a massage therapy course as her Christmas present to Dave, and ministers by massaging his tense back when he comes home after a long day of selling insurance door to door. Fred ministers as he cares for his handicapped wife twenty-four hours a day—doing the cooking, lifting her up to go to the bathroom with a walker, and giving her insulin shots.

Ministry is also reverence for those in need. Paul starts his teaching on marriage and family life by telling us to "defer to one another out of reverence for Christ" (Eph 5:21). Such reverence may be easy in life-giving moments of relationship, but how about times when we try to have power over others to keep them in control? We have too often struggled with headship and subjection rather than intimate partnership, failing to ask forgiveness when we try to have winners and losers in marriage. Sin, as much as beauty and goodness, can occasion real love if we enter into the difficult process of forgiveness and reconciliation.

Mitch Finley writes: "To call marriage a sacrament is to say that one's relationship with God cannot be separated from one's relationship with that bleary-eyed wonder who sits across the breakfast table each morning. In other words, to strive for lasting intimacy with a loving husband or wife means to strive for a loving intimacy with God. Likewise, to make regular time for prayer and a retreat now and then will nourish marital intimacy."[13] The spirituality of marriage is not about long hours of prayer, but about catching a moment for prayer in the bathroom or in the car on the way to work. It is a spirituality of doing what we are called to do with intense love—in the laundry, the kitchen, and the bedroom.

Marriage and family life are not all joy. Often they are scarred by illness, death, abuse, addiction, lack of communication, and the absence of family members due to work and other activities. Yet people look to their home as the primary source of nurturing and the place where they find much of their identity. Home is a place where we are rooted. In the creative tension of family life, we move toward or away from each other.

Families experience themselves as a people deeply blessed and deeply broken. They celebrate the gift of life itself, and the gift of each person, a gift given to them by God to be parent, child, spouse. The family as a church unit deals with inhabiting, human attachments, providing, touching and being touched, welcoming and affirming and shaping lives. Being family allows people to share the giving of life, nurturing and guiding, loving and accepting love, which continues the Creator's plan from generation to generation.

We welcome a child into the home, accepting responsibility for care all day long and every day for many years. We welcome a lifetime of joys and pains in the unfolding mystery of another life, committing ourselves to care for another in sickness, to alter our plans for another's needs, and to allow ourselves to be changed as another calls us from our own self-centeredness. To welcome a child is to find ourself loving in new ways and to find our heart opening to love differently with each new personality. The love we have for those close to us must become transparent enough for the love of God to be seen through it.

Family spirituality means that we have hearts big enough to create a space in which others are welcome and in which they experience their dignity as children of God. The love and service that characterize family life must also spill out into the broader community. We welcome others through hospitality, when we openly embrace others as children of God, recognizing the ties that bind us together as a Christian community. We welcome and share with guests the love and warmth of our family life.

Often we welcome others to the dinner table. To prepare and share a meal together is a holy act. To eat together is to sustain life in community, a moment of communion in which we enact the mystery of our mutual need and nourishment. If we can move beyond conflict or trivial conversation to encounter each other, we help each person to know who they truly are.

When our hearts have opened to love another, they also must be prepared to let go. Letting go of a young adult venturing into the world or a spouse at death does not mean ceasing to love, or detaching ourself from the affection we feel but rather loving more. Letting go means we entrust what we most love and value to the care and protection of God. Being family stretches and tears our hearts as we love beyond our own self.

The love of God and love of spouse and children cannot be separated. Their needs determine our earthly journey. In living in close communion with those people God has placed in our lives, we encounter the Lord. We stand in the presence of God with our arms around those in our care and pray: "God, look kindly upon those persons you have entrusted to me and have mercy."

Reflection: How have I experienced the sacred in our family life? How do I feel about my answer?

Sharing: Since married couples are called to a sacramental lifestyle, how do I see us living out our sacrament daily?

15

What Is Most Important in My Life?

Shawn and Opal's marriage was on the rocks. Both were hurting and wanted out of the relationship, although they did not share their feelings with each other. Ask Shawn what his highest values were and he would immediately answer his family. Opal disagreed. She complained that Shawn was always at work. When he wasn't at work, he was busy with community activities. She never saw him, except when he came home almost ready for bed. In stating that his family was his most important value, Shawn was talking about an ideal rather than a value.

Hidden deep within us are forces and energies which shape our personality and serve as daily guides giving direction to our lives. Our values are part of this powerful potential within us. A *value* is something I recognize as good and worthwhile that I choose to have in my life now by sacrificing other things. Most of us never seriously consider what our true values are, although we think we could easily list them. But whether we discover them or not, they are deep within our being and shape our ideas, feelings, attitudes, and convictions. Our values clearly affect our behavior.

An *ideal* is something I recognize as good and worthwhile that I want in my life sometime in the future. I am not willing to sacrifice for it right now. We often think something is a value because it is important to us. But if we're honest with ourselves, we will find out that we are not willing to sacrifice for it. This suggests that it is an ideal, not a value. For example, James and Mary have longed for a simple lifestyle for a long time, but they can't seem to embrace it in their lives. Our ideals can motivate us in our quest for real values, but they are not values in themselves.

Our moral values are important. Every relationship between two people is a moral relationship, since morality centers on understanding how we can legitimately deal with one another and with our common environment. Moral values are always personal values. We love and hate, are joyful and sorrowful. We reflect moral values through simplicity, generosity, truthfulness, goodness, justice, honesty, peace, joy, courage, and love. These values are developed by a conscious and free surrendering of ourselves.

We find our moral values only when we can go beyond the questions of "What's in it for me?" and look for what is good, true, just, and beautiful. For example, what value do we place on life? We see many couples struggling with the issue of birth control. Often they make their decisions on family planning based on convenience rather than respect for life.

Everyone has values. People who understand their values, seeing the connection between values and actions, act consistently and with commitment. People who know and live by their values have taken conscious steps to develop those values.

Our lifestyle is largely based on our values, on what is most important to us. Our values determine how we deal with such issues as social status, use of money, sex, roles, morality, religion, politics, choice of friends, parenting our children, attitudes toward work and play, and the way we use our leisure time. Traditionally, we think of values as absolutes. If asked to name our values, we often use words such as "honesty," "thrift," or "generosity," or recite mottos such as "It is better to give than to receive." But in the reality of daily living, our values are more difficult to name. Clarifying our values can help us in making daily decisions and choices.

Every day of our lives we make decisions. Some are minor, like whether to visit a friend or to buy a shirt. Others have serious consequences, such as whether to change jobs, have a child, or get a divorce. A clear awareness of our personal values can be the key to reaching the best choice.

All of us have a deeply ingrained value system absorbed from what our families and culture consider "right." We have personal values that we bring into our marriage and other relationships. We also have couple values that both spouses are willing to sacrifice for.

Value conflicts happen between all spouses. Conflicts actually provide important insights when the values and beliefs underneath them are explored. When we are open to learning, the goal is not to discover whose values are right and whose are wrong, but rather to understand the important reasons each spouse has for holding their values and why our actions sometimes contradict our values.

When we have a conflict, we can't resolve that conflict without seeing what is at stake, or the values behind our responses. By prioritizing our values, we can make our conflicts less painful. Some of our values are hidden from us. Our spouse can be helpful in pointing out some of these values. When a couple understands their values they can readily work together on these values.

One way to discover our authentic values is to determine where we spend our time, our money, and our energy, and where we are willing to risk. For example, in the opening story of the chapter, Shawn claimed that his family was his highest value, but he invested more time, energy, and risks in his work.

Values are basic for growth in our relationships. Respecting each other's values does not mean that we have to give up our own. Our values may change as our self-understanding deepens, but we should not be forced to give them up. To give up our values and beliefs under pressure will cause us to lose a sense of ourself.

It is not easy to change our value systems, especially if they are rigid. But questioning our values rather than trying to convince another to believe our way lets us shed values we have outgrown. As we face such decisions, we establish a unique identity by choosing values rather than just absorbing those of our culture.

Values that make daily living personally satisfying and socially constructive are consciously and freely chosen and acted upon consistently. Clarifying our values will help us make self-enhancing rather than self-defeating decisions. This helps shape a vision of the way our life can be in the future, out of which we commit ourself to a course of action. Here are some guidelines for recognizing what we value.

1. We choose what we value from the available alternatives. We can't know or live by our values if we are blind to the alternatives or trapped by barriers. If we don't

understand our options before we make a choice, we risk getting stuck with a life or circumstances we do not desire. A valuable choice is made only after we have explored all the avenues open to us.

2. We choose what we value after considering the consequences. What might we gain and lose by pursuing this alternative? Will our choice lead to what we desire? Will it hurt people around us? What are our own personal strengths and limitations in achieving this alternative?

3. We freely choose what is valuable. We choose without outside pressure or without concern for a reward or punishment, although aware of the wisdom of others.

4. We prize and cherish what we value. A valuable choice, such as giving up smoking, lets us feel good about ourself and gives us a sense of accomplishment and self-worth. At times we are willing to give up something else, like a higher paying job, to keep what we truly value. When values are involved, nothing can steer us off our course, We are ready to fight for a change, putting our time, energy, and emotion into it.

5. We publicly affirm what we value. When we truly value a choice or goal we are ready and willing to talk about it. We admit our values when asked about them in public and voluntarily express our feelings to people willing to listen.

6. A value prompts us to take consistent action. We do something to get and keep what we sincerely desire. If we value parenthood, we choose to have children. We act upon our value by learning to be good parents, and we make certain sacrifices. If we value health, we take action to get healthy and stay healthy. Our behavior is a visible proof of what we value.

7. We act consistently and repeatedly for something we value. We make a commitment and we persevere in difficult as well as easy times. At the first sign of trouble, we do not turn back or give up on what we value. Acting

upon our beliefs again and again, we will be living the life we honestly want to lead.

Clarifying values is hard work and a lifelong process. We never attain perfect clarity or act with perfect consistency, but we can become more decisive. Throughout our lives we have to make choices and live with them. When our choice is based on a true value, we generally complete most or all of the steps mentioned above.

Reflection: What is the most important value in my marriage? Does my behavior reflect this value?

Sharing: What are some of my ideals that I assumed were my values? How do I feel about my answer?

16

Even Roses Have Thorns

"Marriage is anything but boring," writes Ina Hughs in the *Detroit Free Press.*

> She changes dress sizes and hair color and politics. He grows scalp instead of hair, develops an allergy to casseroles and loses an average of two pairs of fingernail clippers a month.
>
> They stand by a crib and quibble over who looks like whom. They hold hands at graduations. They see each other in the same bathrobe, Christmas after Christmas. She discovers he loves gardening, taking long walks by himself and doesn't like anyone to make a fuss over him when he's tired, but expects it when he's sick. He finds out she's scared of moths, dentists, gas grills and missing out on anything. She wishes he'd come right out and say, "Get me some butter," instead of "Do we have any butter?" or "Where's the butter?" or even "Would you like some but-

ter?" It takes a lot of living together to know what it means to love someone.[14]

Roses often symbolize love for us. My gardening experience tells me the rose is an appropriate symbol. The beauty of the rose deceives me into forgetting the painful thorns until I get close. From a distance, I often respond to a newly discovered rose with a profoundly whispered "Wow!" or "Thanks, God!", only to find myself wounded and bleeding when I get too close. Love relationships, like roses, have thorns. Lucky folks enjoy the roses without getting impaled on and damning the thorns.

Steps to Recovery of a Relationship

I have twelve steps that I believe are important for a couple trying to rebuild their relationship. These are not the twelve steps of Alcoholics Anonymous, although some of the steps are similar. While I believe that all of these steps are important, they're not necessarily in a progressive order, nor are they all of equal importance for every couple.

Step 1. *I admit I can't change my spouse and stop blaming my spouse for all my pain.* I need to admit my life has become unmanageable, and that I need to change myself. When I change, my spouse may change.

Most of us don't want to give up control of the other person. Instead, we want our spouse to behave in the way we believe is best. When a marriage runs into difficulty, the natural reaction is to try even harder to control our spouse's behavior.

It takes a lot of strength to admit we are powerless, to see that our spouse is not the sole cause of our pain in the misery stage, and to accept the fact that we cannot change our spouse. When we can do this, it shifts the responsibility for our spouse's behavior on his or her shoulders, where it belongs.

For the healing process to occur, we must accept responsibility for our own actions and behavior. The way to recovery is to embrace our pain, loneliness, and shame. Once we can admit this and find acceptance from others, we can begin to accept ourself.

Step 2. *I need to look at the behavior of the family I grew up in, to discover what unhealthy relationship skills I learned at home, and to understand how this affects my present relationship.* Our parents formed our beliefs about ourselves. If they used abusive and shaming rules, they destroyed our inner identity. We look back not to blame our parents, but to learn about ourselves so that we can grow.

If we do not know our family history, we keep repeating the same behavior. If we were hurt by abusive or manipulative parents from whom we learned our relationship skills, we will pass these behaviors on to our children unless we make significant changes.

Children from unhealthy families approach marriage like empty buckets needing to be filled. Each needy partner has an illusion that the spouse is going to fulfill their incomplete self. Then they entrap each other rather than build a stable relationship.

We need to look back to our family of origin to come to grips with our past, to understand who we are, to forgive our parents, and then to give up the roles or scripts that have given us power or left us powerless.

Step 3: *I take a searching look at myself, seeking to discover the real me.* A lot of people have messed up self-images. Some were shamed, which made them feel worthless. Others suffered abandonment, which led them to develop a false self in order to survive and be accepted. This false self forms a defensive mask that distracts from the pain and inner loneliness of the true self. As adults they are still hiding, feeling alone, afraid to discover the true self. Without self-love, we cannot love another.

We might begin to explore our self-image by asking questions such as:

- ◆ What made me acceptable in the past or now (e.g., service to others)?
- ◆ What makes me feel good (e.g., putting others' needs first, even though I don't take care of my own needs)?
- ◆ What are the sayings I grew up with that now keep playing in my mind (e.g., "I told you so!" or "You're no damn good!")?
- ◆ Have I been able to forgive myself for past mistakes?

Many people react with fright and mistrust when someone says "I love you!" Sometimes others who said they loved them used them instead. Parents may have loved them conditionally, giving the message "I will love you if . . ." More often the fear comes from our inability to love ourselves. The ability to feel good about ourselves—to love, appreciate, and celebrate our own goodness—is basic to our happiness and the key factor in a healthy personality.When true love is missing in our lives, it may be because we have either selfishly or timidly kept the doors of our heart locked and barricaded. We are either unwilling or unable to risk transparency, to expose the most sensitive areas of our soul to another, to seek intimacy. When I love myself, I empower others to love themselves. We are like mirrors to one another.

Step 4: *I need to communicate openly and honestly, especially at the feeling level.* Good communication is the ground for healthy relationships, while bad communication leads to unhealthy relationships. In unhealthy families, parents often do not show their emotions nor do they allow their children to express feelings. Abusive families frequently hide secrets of shame and demand that members repress their feelings. To question is an act of disobedience.

A healthy family provides for the emotional needs of each member. Communication is clear and overt. Openness is a process of talking and listening, which involves elements of trust, risk, and acceptance. I am willing to let you know me and to trust you to accept me. I want to know and accept you as you are. Openness makes us vulnerable, afraid of looking foolish or of being rejected. I talk about the person I really am.

Love grows when I communicate myself to another and diminishes when I close up and withdraw from another. The work of love is to develop a true honesty and transparency with each other.

Step 5: *I need to make the decision to love, to move beyond my misery to recreate a better relationship with my spouse.* As e.e. cummings wrote: "one's not half two. it's two are halves of one." The beginning chapters of the Bible reflect such an insight when they picture male and female together created in the image of God. We are incomplete without each other. We all have a need for love, even if we are so damaged we can't acknowledge or express this need. Love between a man and a woman can and should be the most liberating, maturing, and fulfilling experience of adult human life. However, such love is not easy to achieve.

The most healing experience, and one that most promotes human change and growth, happens in a one-to-one relationship of love. Paul reminds us that such love is not self-seeking. Love asks not "What's in it for me?" but "What can I do for you?" and "Who can I be for you?" Unconditional love can change the life of the person to whom it is offered. The first impulse to change comes not from being challenged but from being loved. Love can be the seed that gradually breaks down the barriers to human relationships.

To love and to accept love is a risk. We all aspire toward the goal of unconditional love, a goal not realistically within our reach in human relationships. To some extent we are all injured, limited by our own scars, needs, and pains. The greatest gift I can give to another is to help that person love himself or herself, as people help me to believe in and love myself. My love must be liberating and not possessive or manipulating. I must allow others to be themselves and not who I want them to be.

Wanting the best for you and trying to be what you need me to be must be done in a way that allows you to have your own feelings, think your own thoughts, and make your own decisions. If I love you, I will carefully and sensitively respect your personhood. Only when you know you are loved can you get to that necessary truth that you are lovable. When you believe that you are lovable, you will come to expect love from others, and be ready to take the risks of loving and being loved.

Step 6: *I need to approach conflict as a learning experience rather than with defensive or self-protective behavior.* Conflict is inevitable in every relationship. I can choose to blame my spouse or I can learn from the experience and practice loving behavior. Often, our best learning experiences come from our conflicts with each other, as we look at our reactions and feelings. A defensive and self-protective path leads to negative consequences, while an open, vulnerable, learning path leads to growth.

Most people believe they love, yet act out of fear. They may attempt to control, getting their spouse to change behavior by creating fear or guilt in that person. They may go along with what the spouse wants out of fear or guilt. Such behaviors are not loving.

When we approach conflict as a learning opportunity, it nurtures emotional and spiritual growth, leading to self-esteem, joy, and intimacy. I am open to learning all I can about what the conflict can teach me. I want to learn primarily about myself and how I can be responsible. I want to learn from my feelings rather than protect them, even if the truth is painful. If I focus primarily on my spouse, this may be a way to protect myself from looking inward. My spouse can help me learn about myself. Openness to learning is always a loving behavior.

Step 7: *I make the decision to trust and to share my feelings.* Trust is the decision I make to let my spouse back into my life at this time. Trust calls me to be open and to share my honest feelings. Hurts and disappointments make it difficult to keep trusting, as does fear of revealing my vulnerability. Rather than let my feelings dictate my behavior, I rise above my feelings and decide to trust. Trust challenges me to accept my spouse's feelings as they are, rather than try to manipulate or to cause my spouse to hide behind a mask.

Concentrating on the goodness I believe is in my spouse helps me make the decision to love. Trust and openness are a conscious deliberate choice. I am willing to change the way I listen, so that I don't cause hurts and build mistrust, and I am willing to share my true self rather than hide behind masks. Trust doesn't just happen; it has to be created. Prayer can be a source of strength in making the decision to trust. An atmosphere of trust is essential to good, intimate communication.

Step 8: *I need to forgive and seek forgiveness to heal the shame that binds me.* Often the hurts that cause barriers seem like little things—a harsh word, failure to listen, cutting in when another is talking, failing to do what I promised for a spouse. It's the little things in life that hurt. You can sit on a mountain top but not on a tack. Forgiveness of these seemingly little hurts is important for a healthy marriage; it needs to happen frequently.

Forgiveness brings about healing. We often carry around a lot of guilt that does us no good. One reason for this guilt is that we haven't experienced and accepted forgiveness. Sometimes we refuse to believe that we are forgiven. Often that happens because a parent or spouse excused our actions rather than forgiving them. To excuse somehow hangs onto the memory of what happened and is really a judgment.

To forgive means to let go of the past and to accept another person without conditions. When I share regret with you for what your failure did to you, rather than make you feel guilty for having done it, I am likely forgiving. Forgiveness seeks to heal the one who failed and now struggles with these failures. A forgiving attitude allows one who is hurt to reach out with forgiveness rather than waiting for the one who did the hurting to come crawling to ask forgiveness. Prayer is important in forgiveness, especially the Lord's Prayer: "Forgive us our trespasses as we forgive those who trespass against us."

Step 9: *Intimacy requires the ability to be vulnerable.* People who have difficulty with intimacy often have no relationship with themselves. They fear abandonment and try to hang on by controlling their spouse. Control is a great enemy of intimacy.

We may yearn for a deeper intimacy, yet we also fear it. We may be afraid to lose our individuality, or afraid our spouse will discover our weakness and reject us. We may remember earlier hurts and not want to risk again. We avoid getting close, even though we yearn for it and need it.

To be intimate is to risk exposing our inner selves to each other, to bare our deepest feelings, desires, and thoughts. It is to be the very person we are, and to love and accept each other unconditionally. Intimacy is the fruit of a mature marriage relationship. Intimacy is the day by day ways we are involved with and show love for each other. It requires that both people make the decision to love and live in the present with intense love. Creating an atmosphere of intimacy requires work, especially healthy listening.

People often connect intimacy only with sexuality, when in truth the degree of intimacy is in proportion to the amount of mutual trust, confidence, and self-revelation in the relationship.

Step 10. *I come to recognize a need for God if I am to recover my marital relationship.* Alcoholics Anonymous tells us to "let go and let God." It is difficult to let go of control, to become powerless over our lives, and to let God take charge. St. Augustine reminds us: "Our hearts are restless until they rest in you, O God." It makes sense to build a relationship with the God who wants us to find happiness in marriage.

Studies tell us that the most significant factor in a successful marriage is the faith life of the couple. And married couples say they most find God in their marriage and family life. Spirituality is wholeness. I begin by developing a deep insight into myself as one made in the image of God, and by a willingness to make the changes in my life that enable me to build healthy relationships.

Prayer is a dialogue with God about how I feel and what I need. Prayer helps me confront my dividedness and strive for healthy answers. When spouses pray together, they let God into their relationship. God is their lifeline. The God we see in Jesus was not busy assuring the saved, but seeking out the broken and hurting folks to bring them to God. Would not that God hear our prayers for healing of our relationships?

Step 11: *I/We need to join a support group.* All married couples face difficult moments and need others with whom they can share. Studies show that couples with healthy marriages tend to have the support of seven or eight other couples with whom they can be open. Hurting couples tend to feel alone, believing no one else has their problems, and they hide the secret of their brokenness. They don't dare to look at themselves, let alone share the pain with others. When we can trust someone else and experience their love and acceptance, we begin to change our beliefs about ourselves.

Certainly the Twelve Step program of Alcoholics Anonymous has shown us the power of groups that allow each person to be real, to openly share feelings, and to find help, hope, and support. People in hurting marriages desperately need a place where they can feel comfortable discussing their misery with others who share similar experiences and understand what they are going through. The bonding helps all members to learn and grow when they can reach gut level sharing.

Healing from brokenness is a long, gradual process and not an overnight miracle. Couples can't do it alone. Questions and fear will linger. Can I change? Will my spouse change? Can I trust again? Can I let go of my guilt? Can I forgive and be forgiven? Support groups remind us that roses can grow out of a pile of garbage.

Step 12: *One of the most important ways to keep our marriage alive is to help others.* We remember how alone we felt and how much strength we gained knowing that there were others who had gone through similar situations. When we were going through the misery, we would not have considered it a grace. Yet now we realize that we could not possibly help other people, or understand what they are going through or feeling, if we had not experienced it ourselves. God speaks through us to others.

I think Susan has learned that she has a gift to offer. In her personal note to me on their Christmas card, Susan said: "We can't thank you enough for encouraging and challenging us . . . you started us on our way. Our third group of couples are almost through the program. They're an interesting group to work with."

I remember when Susan and John in no way believed they could help others because of their own problems. Usually it is not our strength but our brokenness that enables us to become a grace for others.

Scripture tells us: "It is more blessed to give than to receive" (Acts 20:35). What an important lesson for all of us. Anyone who only receives ultimately shrivels or becomes stagnant. The more fortunate, happier people are usually those who are giving as well as receiving. When a couple begin to share their lives with others, they begin to grow. An important part of recovery comes through sharing what we have received.

Love is the tough, essential answer to the riddle of who we are meant to be as human beings. Much of our society reflects a lack of love which causes most of us to be fearful. All of the activity in the divorce courts, the fragmentation of family life, or the failure of parents to be stable and loving make us question the possibility of love in our world, and even the love of God for us. We need to become aware of healthy love relationships that create whole and happy people. Love is hard work; yet it happens if people work at it.

"There is no limit to love's forbearance, to its trust, its hope, its power to endure. Love never fails. . . . Seek eagerly after love" (1 Cor 13).

Reflection: How has the experience of being loved or not being loved shaped my life?

Sharing: What steps am I willing to take to rebuild my marriage?

EPILOGUE

I just spent a weekend with couples who participated in Retrouvaille and are now preparing to help other couples by sharing their stories. While their pain may sometimes overshadow the mystery of grace in their lives, I was deeply aware of God's presence in their midst.

The ecstasy of emotionally and physically rediscovering one's intimate partner and being rediscovered physically and emotionally by one's spouse is a hint of the ecstasy of rediscovering and being discovered by God.

Given the renewed awareness that God has made human love, including sex, sacramental, it is time for the church to speak positively and realistically about the crucial human experience of falling in love again. If couples who have rediscovered their love then reach out to help others, the church will become a place where people find the support they seek for their marriage and family life.

The church is about a people striving to see God. To see God more clearly and to be born in the new ways God wishes for us, we need to be vulnerable to and reflective of the experiences around us, to experience all of life as a central part of the divine mystery.

I believe we experience the movement of God at key and often painful moments in our lives. Yet much of our time and energy is devoted to numbing ourselves to an openness and vulnerability to God's presence and action. To get in touch with the realities of our lives brings us to an experience of ourselves that wrenches us away from a denial that we are in need. It is terribly threatening to be needy, and we avoid it because it asks us to believe in love.

Any birth is difficult. God is asking us to be born through the frustrations, tears, joys, celebrations, laughter, feelings, and experiences of daily life. Those times of uncertainty, when we seek to get deeper into the reality around us, are moments of faith challenging us to believe in ourselves and love and God.

As church, we can do no better than be there for each other in these moments.

NOTES

[1] Quoted by Dan Morris, "Seasons of a Marriage: How to Keep a Good Thing Growing," *U. S. Catholic* (September, 1988), p. 36.

[2] John Paul II, "On the Family" (*Familiaris Consortio*), #86.

[3] Tom and Vivien Hipelius, "Retrouvaille—A Caring Ministry," *Deacon Digest* (Vol. 5, No. 1, February, 1988), p. 13.

[4] *Ibid.*

[5] Ina Hughs, "Dance of the Dinosaurs" (Knight-Ridder Newspapers—*Detroit Free Press*, reprinted in ACT, newsletter of the Christian Family Movement, Vol. 42, No. 2, February, 1989), p. 1.

[6] Quoted by Dan Morris, "Seasons of a Marriage," p. 33.

[7] Associated Press report in *Marriage Partnership* (Fall, 1988), p. 8.

[8] Quoted by Dan Morris, "Seasons of a Marriage," p. 32.

[9] John Powell, *Happiness Is an Inside Job* (Allen, Texas: Tabor Publishing, a division of DLM Inc., 1989), p. 116.

[10] Quoted in *Matrimony* (Vol. 3, No. 2, Spring, 1989), p. 22.

[11] Tom and Vivien Hipelius, "Retrouvaille—A Caring Ministry," p. 11.

[12] Donald Hillstom, "What I Wish I Had Known Before the Divorce," *Minneapolis Star*, November 3, 1991, reprinted with permission from the *Star Tribune*.

[13] Quoted by Dan Morris, "Seasons of a Marriage," p. 35.

[14] Ina Hughs, "Dance of the Dinosaurs," p. 1.